本科学术互认课程
系列教材

U0331695

Academic English Writing, Second Edition

学术英语写作

（第2版）

陈雪　唐利芹　郭旋　徐婧　徐磊　王倩◎编著

清华大学出版社
北京

版权所有，侵权必究。举报：010-62782989，beiqinquan@tup.tsinghua.edu.cn。

图书在版编目 (CIP) 数据

学术英语写作 / 陈雪等编著 . —2 版 . —北京：清华大学出版社，2024.5
本科学术互认课程系列教材
ISBN 978-7-302-66210-5

Ⅰ . ①学… Ⅱ . ①陈… Ⅲ . ①英语－写作－高等学校－教材 Ⅳ . ① H319.36

中国国家版本馆 CIP 数据核字 (2024) 第 086734 号

责任编辑：严曼一
封面设计：李召霞
版式设计：方加青
责任校对：王凤芝
责任印制：刘 菲

出版发行：清华大学出版社
  网　　　址：https://www.tup.com.cn，https://www.wqxuetang.com
  地　　　址：北京清华大学学研大厦 A 座　　　　　邮　　编：100084
  社 总 机：010-83470000　　　　　　　　　　　邮　　购：010-62786544
  投稿与读者服务：010-62776969，c-service@tup.tsinghua.edu.cn
  质 量 反 馈：010-62772015，zhiliang@tup.tsinghua.edu.cn
印 装 者：三河市铭诚印务有限公司
经　　销：全国新华书店
开　　本：185mm×260mm　　印　　张：14　　　字　　数：285 千字
版　　次：2020 年 8 月第 1 版　2024 年 5 月第 2 版　印　次：2024 年 5 月第 1 次印刷
定　　价：79.00 元

产品编号：102112-01

Preface

In accordance with the guiding ideology of "deepening the reform of higher education through the internationalization of education" in the "Outline of National Medium and Long-Term Education Reform and Development Program(2010-2020)", *Academic English Writing* is mainly designed for International Scholarly Exchange Curriculum (Undergraduates) (ISEC), and it is also applicable to non-English majors and learners who intend to study abroad. This textbook is mainly to help ISEC undergraduates to understand the international English academic writing norms and basic requirements, to help them successfully complete the academic English writing, research reports and other writing tasks. It also creatively guides students to flexibly apply critical thinking abilities and skills into academic writing, enabling students to express their academic ideas by using standard language.

Academic English Writing mainly focuses on explaining the main steps of writing process, the related requirements and methods of academic writing. It is composed of 12 units, each of which involves the structure and skills of academic English expository and argumentative writing. This textbook mainly discusses the sections of academic writing, including topic selection, material collection and evaluation, outline writing, article cohesion and transition, language style characteristics, writing norms, reference notes, publishing process, acknowledgments and so on. In addition, the appendixes contain a format guide of the references and the notes related to the academic writing.

The editors of this textbook are all the backbone teachers active in the front-line teaching of colleges and universities. They are composed of six teachers, from Jilin Normal University, Inner Mongolia University for Nationalities, Guizhou University of Finance and Economics, Chifeng University and other universities. According to the development trend of ISEC undergraduates' professional disciplines, the editors have carried out a special research around the existing excellent teaching materials and structures, and reflected the feasibility and applicability of critical thinking ability in editing the writing materials.

In the course of compiling the textbook, we (editors) have read and consulted many related works, textbooks and online materials, and hereby we would like to express our sincere thanks to all the relevant authors. In addition, the office of ISEC has invited experts to strictly review and control the quality of the structure and content of this textbook. Grateful acknowledgement to all in particular!

Due to the limited knowledge level of editors, there are inevitably some problems in the book. Criticism and corrections from readers are warmly welcomed.

Editors

May 2024

序 言

遵循《国家中长期教育改革和发展规划纲要（2010—2020）》"通过教育国际化，深化高等教育改革"的指导思想，《学术英语写作》主要针对国际本科学术互认课程 [International Scholarly Exchange Curriculum (Undergraduates)，ISEC] 而编排设计，同时也适用于非英语专业本科生和希望留学的学习者。本书主要帮助 ISEC 学生了解国际英语学术写作规范和基本要求，有助于学习者顺利完成在专业课学习中所涉及的论文撰写、研究报告等方面的学术英语写作任务，创造性地引导学生在写作时灵活运用思辨能力及技能，使学生能运用规范的语言表达自己的学术思想。

《学术英语写作》围绕学术论文写作的主要步骤、相关要求及方法展开，由十二个单元组成，每个单元都涉及学术英语说明文和论说文写作的结构和技能。本书主要从学术英语论文写作选题、材料收集与评估、提纲撰写、文章衔接与过渡、语言文体特点、写作规范、参考文献的标注、出版流程以及答辩致谢等方面加以详细分述。此外，附录包含参考文献常用格式指南以及论文写作的相关注意事项。

本书的编者都是活跃在教学一线的高校骨干教师，由来自吉林师范大学、内蒙古民族大学、贵州财经大学、赤峰学院等高校的六位教师组成。根据 ISEC 学生的专业学科发展趋势，编者围绕现有优秀教材和结构进行了专题研究，在本书的编写中体现出思辨能力在写作中的可行性和应用性。

在本书的编写过程中，我们参阅了许多相关著作、教材和网上资料，在此向各相关作者致以真诚的感谢！此外，国际本科学术互认课程办公室（ISEC 办）邀请专家们对本书的结构和内容严把质量关，特在此表示感谢！

由于编者水平有限，书中难免有不足之处，希望读者批评指正。

编者
2024 年 5 月

Contents

Chapter 1

Review of Writing Process

In this chapter, you will know:

√ Reasons of writing academic essays,

√ Features of academic writing,

√ Types of support in academic essays,

√ Writing process.

Critical Thinking Questions

Directions: Work in small groups and discuss the following open questions.

■ What is academic writing? Can you list some differences between general writing and academic writing?

General Writing	Academic Writing

■ What are the major reasons why college students write academic essays?

■ What are the general types to support or develop academic paragraphs or essays? (e.g.) cause/effect

■ What kinds of possible punishments will be given for academic plagiarism? Please list them and tell the reasons.

② Introduction to Academic Writing

Academic writing is a formal style of writing which is done by students or scholars. The main purpose of academic writing is to inform and not to entertain like novels. Both academic writers and academic readers are eager to know the useful information they are looking for in academic writings. Academic writing is often complex and abstract, partly due to the academic subject matter and academic language itself.

Usually, academic writing can take many forms: journal articles, essays, theses, group project reports, research reviews, and etc. Although college students are increasingly being asked to write in different forms, the formal-essay or dissertation (paper) still remains the most popular type of academic writing. Essays written by students are likely to be read by their tutors as the assignment form. The essay can be set as a coursework assignment to assess a student's understanding of a subject, or as an exam question. And thesis (paper) is written by students as an evaluation of student college study in four academic years.

Features of academic writing

A written piece of academic work is linear, which means it has one recognizable central subject or theme. It relates to the craftsmanship of certain rules and procedures of correct quoting and evidencing of sources, with a precise formulation of objectives. As well, it is in the standard written form of the language, without digressions or repetitions. Consequently, there are five main features of academic writing as follows. (Els Van Geyte, 2013)

拓展阅读: 1.1

Basic Information
for Research Paper

(1) Complexity

Academic written language is relatively more complex. It is lexically denser and it has a more varied vocabulary. It uses more noun-based phrases than verb-based phrases. Usually, written texts have long complex sentences, and the language has more grammatical complexity, including more subordinate clauses and more passives.

(2) Formality/Objectivity

Academic writing is relatively formal and its written language is usually objective rather than personal. In general, the student should avoid colloquial words and expressions. Further, it has impersonal tone, usually avoiding some intimacy words such as "you", "we" or "I", but rather using "he", "she", "researcher", and so on. It can also be understood as avoiding subjectivity.

(3) Clarity

Academic writing is explicit about the relationships in written texts. Furthermore, the academic writer or student should be responsible to make it clear to the readers how the various parts of the text are related. These connections can be made clear by the use of different signaling words. Simply, the ideas and information are explicit, accurate and precise.

(4) Coherence

Academic writing should be coherent about text parts and paragraph sentences. Coherence means unmistakably clear and reasonable connection between academic parts or paragraphs and their relationships. In academic essays, coherence implies the orderly progression of facts and ideas in logic and consistent sequence, and writers usually use transitional signals, substitution of pronouns, parallelism and logical order to achieve writing coherence.

(5) Responsibility

In academic writing, students must be responsible and be able to provide evidence and justification for any claims or statements they make. Students are also responsible for demonstrating the understanding of any source texts they use. They need to document and reference for any information included in academic writing — do not plagiarize.

Activity 1 »

Directions: Work with a partner. Discuss and evaluate which of the following sentences are academic language, and which are colloquial language. Write changes that would make them stronger academic language.

(1) In my opinion, this is very interesting.

(2) You can easily know how different life was 50 years ago.

(3) Human beings are inherently competitive, eager to be happy.

(4) Whenever I'd visited there before, I'd ended up feeling that it would be a miracle.

(5) We don't really know what language proficiency is, but many people have talked about it for a long time.

(6) Some economists have recommended taking some measures against financial crisis.

(7) As Hill (2008) observed, human beings are inherently competitive.

(8) It is easy to know how different life was 50 years ago.

(9) By 2014, over 111,000 Saudi students had been studying in the United States, and the number continually increased.

(10) It may be said that the commitment to some social and economic concepts was less strong than it is now.

(11) Researchers have suggested ways of making second language teaching and testing more "communicative" (Canale & Swain, 1979) on the grounds that a communicative approach better reflects the nature of language proficiency.

(12) Many participants in the study reported that they slept well while they had a job to work, but experienced more sleep disruption after they retired.

Activity 2 »

Directions: Work in a small group and discuss these open-answered critical thinking questions.

(1) What are the distinctions between academic essays on Arts and Science?

(2) What are the differences between English academic papers and Chinese academic papers?

3 Review: Types of Support in Academic Essays

If an academic essay is well written and organized, its academic parts or paragraphs should be supported by some methods. Normally, academic writing requires that writers support their ideas and opinions with these supporting details:

a) Related examples

b) A comparison with a similar situation

c) A contrast of opposite situation

d) Quotations from experts

e) Facts

f) Statistics or other numerical data

g) Common knowledge

h) Causes/effects to explain

i) Definition

j) Classification

k) Logical reasoning

l) Personal knowledge

拓展阅读: 1.2

Introduction
to Paragraph
Development

Consequently, good writers will get these kinds of supporting details from outside sources such as books, magazines, newspapers, websites and personal interviews. Also, writers may find it necessary to use a combination of methods in academic writing in order to support their ideas in a well-organized and cohesive manner.

Activity 3 »

Directions: Read the academic essay below. After reading, work with a partner and answer the following questions.

   (1) How many major points are there in this academic essay? What are they?

   (2) What kinds of supporting methods are used by the writer in the essay? Please underline and explain them.

Coca is Not the Enemy

—— Elizabeth Leontiev

To most people, the word *cocaine* evokes images of the illegal white powder and those who abuse it, yet the word has a different meaning to the coca farmers of South America. *Erythroxylum coca*, or the tropical coca plant, has been grown in the mountainous regions of Colombia, Bolivia, and Peru since 3000 BC. The coca plant has been valued for centuries by indigenous South American cultures for its ability to alleviate pain and combat fatigue and hunger (Forero, "Bolivia's Knot"). Just as many Americans drink coffee every day, natives of the Andes Mountains chew coca leaves and drink coca tea for a mild stimulant effect. Easy to grow, not addictive, and offering many medicinal benefits, coca is part of the everyday lives of the people in this region.

Aside from its medical and cultural value, coca is also important to Andean farmers economically, as a result of a long history of illegal drug trafficking. Dried coca leaves mixed with lime paste or alkaline ashes produce cocaine — a highly addictive substance that delivers euphoric sensations accompanied by hallucinations (Gibson). Supplying the coca for the illegal drug trade accounts for a tremendous portion of the Bolivian, Peruvian, and Colombian economies. In Bolivia, for example, it has been estimated that coca makes up anywhere from one-third to three-quarters of the country's total exports (Kurtz-Phelan, 108). In 1990, the Bolivian president even asserted that 70% of the Bolivian gross domestic product was due to the coca trade (Kurtz-Phelan, 108).

Despite such statistics, for most farmers in the region growing coca is about making a living and supporting their families, not becoming wealthy or furthering the use of cocaine. More than half of Bolivians live in poverty, with a large portion earning less than $2 a day (the U.S. Foreign Affairs, Defense, and Trade Div. 2). In the words of one coca farmer, "the U.S. says 'Coca is cocaine, coca is cocaine,' but it isn't," says Argote. "Coca is the tree of the poor" (qtd. In Schultz and Gordon). Can we reduce cocaine trafficking without eliminating coca? Evo Morales, the current president of Bolivia, believes the answer is "yes" and has advocated a "zero cocaine, not zero coca" policy in his country. This policy would allow native Andeans to maintain their cultural practices, boost South American economies, and channel coca into a new market, away from cocaine traffickers. For all of these reasons, the Morales plan should become a model for other coca-growing countries.

Morales gained recognition for his "zero cocaine, not zero coca" program during his 2005 presidential campaign. His policy aims to legalize the coca crop but not the cocaine that is produced from that crop. He also expressed a desire to get the United Nations to rescind its 1961 convention declaring coca an illegal narcotic. In December 2005, Morales won the election with over 50% of the vote, and made history as the first indigenous Bolivian president (Forero, "Coca").

Morales's plan promotes the best interests of the Andean farmers and offers multiple economic and social benefits. First, South American countries would be able to export non-narcotic coca-based products, such as soaps, toothpaste, tea, alcohol, and candies (Logan). Products like these are already being produced for local use in Bolivia, and manufacturers would like to seek an international market for them. These new coca products would stimulate the Bolivian economy and put money in the pockets of coca growers to support their families, rather than in the pockets of the drug lords. Second, if the market for legal coca were to increase, farmers would be able to make a legal living from a crop that has long been a mainstay of their culture. With legal coca products, the indigenous people of the Andes would not have to sacrifice their way of life. Finally, an increase in the demand for legal coca products might also result in less cocaine being trafficked illegally around the world, since more of the raw material for cocaine will be used for new legal coca products.

In order to understand the benefits of Morales's plan, we must first investigate the failures of the alternatives. The United States has been waging various "wars on drugs" for decades, spending up to $1 billion trying to control cocaine trafficking from South America (Forero, "Bolivia's Knot"). In the 1990s, the United States shifted its efforts from fighting the trafficking of cocaine to eliminating the source of the drug—the coca plants growing in Bolivia, Columbia, and Peru. Coca eradication has taken two main forms. In Bolivia, bands of soldiers move through the countryside, using machetes to hack away coca plants. This process is slow and dangerous, and there have been reports of human rights abuses and extreme violence against the peasant farmers who grow coca (Gordon 16). In nearby Columbia, the United States funded aerial fumigation programs to poison the coca fields; native farmers complain that the herbicide used in the fumigation is causing health problems and environmental pollution ("the U.S. Weight Cost"). By destroying coca plants in Colombia, the United States has "left 500 million people poorer" (Padgett 8). It is unclear whether fumigation results in any benefit, since farmers respond by moving farther and farther into the jungle and replanting their crops there (Otis). Such dense areas are harder to see and therefore harder to fumigate effectively.

Another the U.S. effort encouraged farmers to replace coca with other crops, like coffee, bananas, and pineapples. Alternative crop programs seem like a good idea because they will get rid of the coca farms, but they have own drawbacks. First, as coca grower Leonida Zurita-Vargas noted in her 2003 *New York Times* opinion column, transporting heavy fruits like pineapples from the mountainous coca-growing regions was expensive and difficult. Second, growers are seldom willing to give up coca farming because they can make more money by selling coca than any other crop. Even with government incentives for alternative cropping, coca remains more profitable, a big inducement for poor farmers who can barely support their families and send their children to school. The Houston Chronicle reports that even in areas where farmers have planted alternative crops, the farmers are being lured back to the coca plant by larger profits (Otis). One coca farmer asserted that by growing coca, he could "make ten times what he would make by growing pineapples or yucca" (Harman). Ultimately, alternative cropping means less coca production overall, which will drive up coca prices and encourage more farmers to abandon their alternative crops and return to coca.

After decades of legislation and various eradication programs, cocaine trafficking remains a major problem. The most recent data show that coca cultivation throughout the region remains steady. Contrary to dire predictions, there has been no major spike in Bolivian coca production since Morales was elected at the end of 2005. Furthermore, critics argue that cocaine is no less available in the United States than before eradication began, and street prices remain low (Forero, "Columbia's Coca"). Instead of curbing cocaine trafficking, America's war on drugs has turned out to be a war against the peasants of Colombia, Bolivia, and Peru.

Throughout the years, the various wars on drugs have failed to produce effective results for the United States. The programs of alternative cropping and eradication did not succeed due to the legislators' inability to see life through the eyes of the coca farmers—something Evo Morales was able to do. In 2006, Morales addressed the UN General Assembly and waved a coca leaf in the air, "This is a green coca leaf, it is not the white of cocaine. This coca leaf represents Andean culture; it is a coca leaf that represents the environment and the hope of our peoples." Through his bold program of "zero cocaine, not zero coca", Morales aims to improve the lives of Andean farmers and the economies of South American countries, while still remaining committed to controlling the illegal drug trade. Morales's example illustrates that it is time to work with coca farmers, rather than against them.

4 Plagiarism

Before creating an academic work, college students or academic writers must provide evidence and draw on sufficient information sources of other researchers to the readers. They need to document for any information they include in academic writing.

In Webster online dictionary,

"plagiarism/'plā-jə-, ri-zəm/" (noun) means:

1) an act or instance of plagiarizing;

2) Something plagiarized.

"Plagiarize" is to be defined as:

1) to steal and pass off (the ideas or words of another) as one's own;

2) to use (another's production) without crediting the source;

3) to commit literary theft;

4) to present as new and original an idea derived from an existing source.

扩展阅读: 1.3

Plagiarism

Do not plagiarise. So, what is plagiarism?

Many people think plagiarism is copying another person's work or borrowing someone else's original words or ideas. But simple terms like "copying or borrowing" cannot clarify the seriousness of plagiarism.

As is seen, plagiarism is one act of using someone else's work or ideas or words without giving that person credit. In other words, plagiarism is an act of fraud. It involves both stealing someone else's work and lying about it afterward.

Even after you study a definition of plagiarism in online dictionary, it is not easy to define and judge plagiarism precisely. Additionally, different cultures have different definitions of what constitutes plagiarism in academic settings.

However, for universities or research institutions, they have set various definitions of plagiarism consequences. Possibly, these can be found in different institutions' websites or official documentations.

Activity 4 »

Directions: Work in small groups. Read the following list of punishments for academic plagiarism. Discuss: a) Which of these are used in universities or academic institutions? b) Which are used in companies or larger social institutions? c) Which are used both? Give examples to illustrate.

(1) Failure of one assignment

(2) A warning from a professor

(3) Expelling from one course

(4) Loss of bachelor degree

(5) Expulsion from college or university

(6) A monetary fine

(7) A legal penalty

(8) Banning to enroll in academic institution

(9) Loss of entire academic career

(10) Being sued for plagiarism

(11) Limited or destroyed career opportunities

(12) Failure of paper

(13) Suspension from college or university

(14) Prison

Consequently, every student should be ethically and legally obligated to give credit and acknowledge to another person's ideas or words. For academic writing, most cases of plagiarism can be avoided for students by citing sources. There are some common methods to avoid plagiarism.

Methods to avoid plagiarism:

1) Express your own idea in your own way and in your own words.

2) Use some "common knowledge" as information even if you have learned by researching.

3) Paraphrase what you have read in order to avoid directly copying from the source.

4) Quote directly by giving credit.

5) Provide clear references to all sources quoted or cited.

6) Document all sources quoted in the reference section.

Simply, acknowledging that certain material has been borrowed and providing your readers with the information source, students can easily avoid plagiarism. The two safest methods to avoid plagiarism are: 1) to avoid them altogether, and 2) to paraphrase, quote or cite them properly. Please read Chapter 7 for more information about how to cite or quote information sources properly.

Activity 5 »

Directions: Work with a partner and discuss how to avoid plagiarism for the following extracts.

(1) Women give birth to children and still do most of the work of bringing them up. To do a demanding job of managing family and social life simultaneously is extremely difficult for women (Wajcman, 1981).

(2) Data show that women professionals still assume the primary responsibility of home and child-care activities (Googins and Burden, 1987; Jick and Mitz, 1985).

(3) Career women in India had work and family dilemmas, which are often different from those reported by women in the West (Sekarn, 1992).

⑤ Writing Process of Academic Writing

Brainstorming: Academic writing terms

These words are important for understanding the academic writing process. Work in small groups and match each word with the correct definition.

a. topic	1) A short piece of writing, at least three-para long.
b. edit	2) To change or correct a piece of writing.
c. brainstorm	3) A subject; what the piece of writing is about.
d. organize	4) To arrange in a clear, logical way.
e. proofread	5) To check a piece of writing for errors.
f. revise	6) A first version of a written work.
g. draft	7) Put forward as many ideas as one can think of.
h. essay	8) Judge the worth of some information sources.
i. review	9) A plan for a piece of writing in which each new idea or fact is separately written down.
j. publish	10) Read for errors.
k. outline	11) A careful examination of a situation or process.
l. evaluate	12) Have work printed and be available to the public.

When writing, students do more than just put words together to make sentences or just search some information from Internet. The reason is that academic writing is a process and not a one-shot act. Thus, the writing process of academic writing usually has the following general principles (Allan Glantthorn, 1991):

1) Being complex with involving memory, cognition, language, and psychomotor behaviors.

2) Being multiphase with involving several different stages and many sub-processes, like drafting and revising.

3) Being recursive and interactive with each stage related closely and affected by each other.

To create effective academic essays, good writers must spend time extracting information and thinking critically. This means that strong academic writing process begins with solid planning, having different stages from the start to final draft.

Generally, the process of academic writing is divided into six steps or stages: 1) brainstorming and choosing a topic, 2) doing research and evaluating information, 3) organizing ideas and developing an outline, 4) writing the first draft, 5) reviewing and revising the first draft, and 6) editing the final draft and publishing.

1) The first step is **brainstorming and choosing a topic**. This means that students should intensely but randomly think about the topic, make a list of appropriate ideas, design a word map, and discuss with partners or teachers to make a quick decision about the topic. It is advisable to go from the general to the specific in choosing a topic. An inappropriate topic may lead to the failure of the whole academic essay or at least a waste of time.

2) The second step is **doing research and evaluating information sources**. After choosing a topic, students will think about what they will write about that topic. Next, students will identify an audience and the purpose for

writing, determine the appropriate form for the piece, and then gather ideas and data. Decide and evaluate which of the ideas they want to use and where they want to use them. Choose and circle which idea to talk about first or last; cross out inappropriate ideas.

3) The third step is **organizing ideas and developing an outline**. After choosing a topic and researching deeply, students will know to choose which idea to talk about first, which to talk about next and which to talk about last. Organize the useful ideas and then write an outline logically. If the outline is very detailed, students will write the first draft quickly and smoothly, otherwise failure of written essays will be possible.

4) The fourth step is **writing the first draft**. During the drafting stage, students will write their essay from start to end. Use the finished outline and notes to get their ideas down. They should search for words and try out pieces of sentences and think about paragraph shape. A "free flow" of ideas is encouraged, without letting concern about correct spelling, punctuation, and grammar get in the way of composing. Students need to be aware that the first draft is not a finished product and that any piece of writing can be improved. It is advised that drafting must be done, as far as possible, in one sitting.

5) The fifth step is **reviewing and revising the first draft**. During this stage, students should review the written work's structure and content. Check and revise what they have written, looking for errors, rethinking choices, trying out other words and sentence forms. Totally, students will revise the whole written structure and content, involving adding, substituting, deleting, and moving ideas and words around as writers rework and polish their pieces. They might need to explain something more clearly, or add more details. They may even need to change the organization so that the written text is more logical. Also, read your writing silently to yourself or share with a friend. Getting a reader's opinion is a good way to know if your writing is clear and effective.

6) The final step of the writing process is **editing the final draft and publishing**, which occurs when a completed text is reworked and revised. Editing is the process of getting the piece ready for the audience. The writer is expected to read the text again and make final corrections. Editing can appear in different layers — editing for clarity of ideas and language, editing for grammar conventions, or editing for punctuation, mechanics, and spelling. In other words, editing is a proofreading by the author before the write-up is ready for publication. When a completed text is reworked and edited to the satisfaction of the author, publishing written essay may be possible. However, publishing can appear in various forms, such as submission to the tutor, presentation to the colleagues, or submission to the publisher.

Activity 6 »

Directions: Work in small groups. Complete the chart together and review to summarize the six steps of academic writing process.

Prewriting

Step One: Choose _____

_____

Step Two: Do _____

_____

Step Three: Develop _____

_____

Drafting

Step Four: Write _____

_____

Reviewing and revising

Step Five: Review _____

_____

Revise _____

_____

Editing and publishing

Step Six: May need to do:

Clarify: _____

_____

_____

_____

Submit:_____

_____

_____

_____

Activity 7 »

Directions: Work in a small group and give your presentation to other group members according to the following questions. Your presentation should be given in the PowerPoint form and you should have a good cooperation with group members.

(1) Think of a creative writing process involving the six steps. The topic is the one which you are interested, such as planning a holiday, cooking a meal, friendship, the value of social relationship, writing a poem, decorating a room, surfing internet, online shopping, and WeChat.

(2) Write a short description of what a student would do for each step of academic writing process. For example, at the first step of academic writing, the student presenter should describe carefully how he will brainstorm and choose a suitable subject, which is connected with online shopping.

6 Self-Evaluation

For each statement below, circle the word which is true for you.

1. I understand what academic writing is.	Agree	Disagree	Not sure
2. I know the features of academic essays.	Agree	Disagree	Not sure
3. I know the differences between informal writings and academic writings.	Agree	Disagree	Not sure
4. I understand the writing process or procedure.	Agree	Disagree	Not sure
5. I know useful support types in academic essays.	Agree	Disagree	Not sure
6. I can find key words in titles and understand what I am expected to write.	Agree	Disagree	Not sure
7. I know whom to visit in university if I need advice about an academic essay.	Agree	Disagree	Not sure
8. I know punishments for academic plagiarism.	Agree	Disagree	Not sure
9. I know how to choose an appropriate topic.	Agree	Disagree	Not sure
10. I understand what revision is.	Agree	Disagree	Not sure

Chapter 2

Choosing a Title and Types of Academic Writing

In this chapter, you will know:

√ Principles and purposes of choosing a title,

√ Methods of choosing a title,

√ Standards of good titles,

√ Formats for writing titles.

1 Critical Thinking Questions

Directions: Work in small groups. Discuss the following open questions and share your ideas with classmates.

■ What kinds of issues are shown in the pictures? Are these issues related to people in your country or to you personally?

■ From these social issues shown in the pictures, can you freely brainstorm a title for each of them? Explain the reasons why you choose it.

Purposes of Choosing a Title

When faced with an academic writing assignment, some beginners are passive and think it is a tough problem for them. These beginners say, "What should I write about? What do I know about the topic? Is my topic too broad? Where can I find more information? How can I begin putting some ideas together?" So choosing a title is the first important step in academic writing for college students. At the starting point of academic writing, it is essential to decide the academic value of research paper and to bear the success or failure of research writing.

Choosing a title usually helps to fulfill the following purposes:

(1) Attracting the readers' attention and interest,

(2) Determining the academic value of the research paper,

(3) Indicating the direction, perspective and scale of the paper,

(4) Helping information retrieval of the needed resources,

(5) Providing the writer's layout and review.

扩展阅读: 2.1

Selecting a Topic

In short, in preparing for writing, beginning writers have to decide on a topic, and determine the appropriate form for the pieces. As Ziegler said, "During this time, an embryo is forming; you may not know what, but you sense that something alive will emerge "(1981).

Activity 1 ≫

Directions: Work with a partner. Discuss the purposes of choosing these titles and share your ideas with the whole class.

(1) Shakespeare's Tragedies — On Hamlet's Insanity

(2) Teenage Fashions

(3) A Comparative Study of the Themes in Li Bai's and Du Fu's Poems

(4) Sino-American Relations: 1949-1972

(5) A Favorite Place to Relax

3 Principles for Choosing a Title

To start writing a research paper, beginning writers need a good reason to do it. They will have something they want or need to say. That is, the first point of academic writing is to select a suitable title as a direction to begin free-writing. The title will be the focus of the whole academic paper. How to choose?

Generally speaking, the title you choose for your research papers/essays should be interesting, useful, valuable, researchable, and possible to write about.

(1) Valuable principle

The topic or title selected for your research paper can not be a subject of simple common sense, but rather one of research value.

(2) Scientific and researchable principle

The title of research paper must be scientific, exploring the researchable truth, revealing scientific laws, and applying scientific methods to interpret the facts with strict logic.

(3) Innovative principle

The selection of the title should reflect the novelty and uniqueness of the research paper. Innovation is the soul of academic papers.

(4) Feasible principle

In choosing a title, one should consider subjective and objective conditions, like the practical use of the topic, writer's professional background and writing skills, readers' interest, research materials, and so on.

Besides, in the process of title selection, you can select a subject for yourself. It ought to interest you, and interest others as well, at least potentially. It should be within the range of your

experience and skill, though it is best if it stretches you. It ought not to be too personal, too outdated, and too pedantic. It should be neither so vast that no one can encompass it, nor so narrow and trivial that no one cares. Don't be afraid to express your own opinions and feelings. You are a vital part of the subject.

Activity 2 »

Directions: Work with a partner. Please evaluate the following titles against principles for choosing a title. Tell how to revise them.

(1) Ecotourism

(2) Utilization of Marsh Gas for the Countryside

(3) Food Safety Problems in China

(4) Lady Wang—The Witch or the Normal Girl?

(5) Investigation on Students' Study Motivation Towards Own Majors

(6) A Favorite Part-time Job for Students on Campus

(7) Exploring the Korean Wave from the Hit Song: Gangnam Style

4 Ways of Choosing a Title

Before drafting a research paper, you need to explore a subject, looking for a suitable topic. Usually, you will take some steps to do so.

Step 1: Ask questions to find a topic

To start one's own research basis and expertise, you can consider some general questions to find interesting and researchable topics. It is not likely that all of these questions will be equally applicable, but usually five or six of them will lead to finding a suitable topic.

What? How? When?

Why? What caused it? What were the reasons?

How can the subject be defined?

What does it imply?

What is it different from?

What are its advantages or virtues?

What are its limits or defects?

What do you know about the subject?

What examples are there?

Are there exceptions and qualifications?

Can the subject be analyzed into parts or aspects?

Can these parts be grouped in any way?

Can it retrieve additional information?

Activity 3 »

Directions: Work in small groups or individually, and discuss a favorite topic by using ways of asking questions for finding a suitable title. Please write and share your ideas or questions in the following tables.

Topic 1	Topic 2	Topic 3

Step 2: Brainstorm and map the selected topic

Brainstorming is a way of gathering ideas about a topic. When you brainstorm one selected topic, write down every idea that comes to your mind. Now, don't worry about whether the ideas are good or simple, useful or not. Keep going; jot down everything in your mind about the selected topic. Generally, you will use two methods to brainstorm the selected topic: making a list or mapping.

1) **By making a list**, you can write down anything that occurs to you in single words, phrases or short sentences. Without worrying about order or even making much sense, you are gathering as many ideas as you can. Look at this sample list a student made when brainstorming ideas to write about her topic, "*Study at University* ".

History—learning about the past

Maths (too difficult, not interesting?)

What job do I want later?

English for work? Travel?

Writing is useful?

Science—biology, chemistry

I don't like physics.

Journalism

I like reading literature?

Literature is interesting.

Art—drawing, painting, oil painting, sculpture

Studying/homework

Friends/ social life

2) **Mapping** is the visual presentation of cognitive moves. The writer can use a whole sheet of paper, and place the topic in the middle, with circles or boxes around it. Then write one word or phrase to show the next idea in a circle, and then connect the circles with lines or arrows. The example below shows a mind mapping of "What should I Study?".

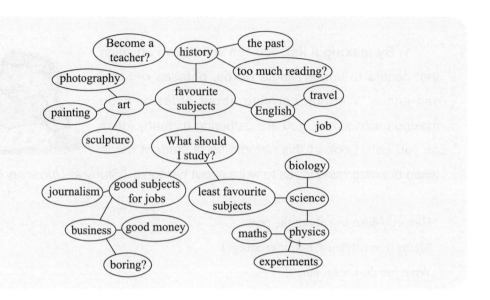

Activity 4 »

Directions: Choose one of the topics below. Brainstorm and make a list of ideas about the topic in five minutes. And then share your ideas with your partner.

(1) An Interesting City

(2) Culture Shock

(3) Marriage

(4) Family Life

(5) Schooling

(6) Advertising

1. _____

2. _____

3. _____

4. _____

5. _____

6. _____

7. _____

8. _____

9. _____

Activity 5 »

Directions: Brainstorm one of the topics below, and make a mind-mapping to list every idea about the topic in five minutes. And then share ideas with your partner.

1. Saving Energy

2. Home Insulation

3. Room Decoration

4. Memories of a Summer Place

5. Computer Revolution

6. Popular Music

7. Campus Crime

8. Family Pets

9. Education

Step 3: Narrow and formulate the final title

Through brainstorming, you possibly have some ideas about the selected topic, but these jotted ideas are not finely reasoned judgments. Many of the ideas are speculative and hastily generalized; some are probably biased. The next task would be to look at them closely, rejecting some, and choosing others. At this time, you should narrow down the scope of your selected topic to formulate a final feasible title. For this, your title must:

Not be too broad or general. Your research paper or essay is of limited length, so you can only focus on one aspect of the selected topic for your paper.

Not be too narrow. You are asked to present a full discussion of the title, so the title must be possible to develop logically and orderly.

Be serious and interesting. You can have natural passion and a reason to write on one title, and you probably know the title is interesting to your readers. You also choose the title that is important. As you are doing serious academic work, you must show depth and insight in your analysis. Your paper must make people think and learn.

Be something within the range of your abilities. No matter how fascinated you may be with the title, you need to write your essay from your own training or knowledge. If you have no training in physics, you will not know how to say about space flight.

Be sufficient in valuable materials. The views in a research paper should usually be supported by a variety of sources. That is, you need to find out more information about the title, and find information easily.

Be objective, not personal or subjective. The final title should be treated objectively in research papers, which is not involving personal likes and dislikes. Nor will you discuss the point subjectively, seldom using "I" or "We".

Activity 6 »

Directions: Work with a partner and follow the directions of ways to narrow the topics. Please develop a final title and freely introduce your writing ideas on the following topics. You should choose two topics to discuss freely.

1. Saving Energy

2. Home Insulation

3. Room Decoration

4. Memories of a Summer Place

5. Computer Revolution

6. Popular Music

7. Campus Crime

8. Family Pets

9. Internet

10. Formal Education

11. Drama

12. Biology

5 Types of Academic Writing

After choosing a final title, you should know what types of academic writings expected to write. In the college, academic writings can be of various types, including empirical research, review papers, journals and full length thesis, but briefly it takes the form of research papers. Such research papers get broadly divided into two categories, namely, ***conceptual research papers*** and ***empirical research papers***.

- **Conceptual research papers**, also called expository papers, explain or describe or document a research activity, only by presenting facts or a synthesis of existing research works. It does not involve testing or first-hand test data, not having the writer's opinion about the topic.

- **Empirical research papers**, also called persuasive papers, document the process and the outcome of *research hypotheses* by methods, including research process, data collection and analysis, etc.

Additionally, empirical research papers still contain facts or theories, but they aim to convince the reader to have an attitude or take a certain action. A conceptual paper usually informs, not to change behavior or beliefs.

Activity 7 »

Directions: Work in small groups. Complete the chart together and check whether the topics below are for a conceptual essay/research paper or for an empirical essay/research paper. Explain your ideas to your group.

Titles	Conceptual essay	Empirical essay
1. The Effects of Cell Phone on the Body		
2. An Investigation of Students' Motivation of Studying English		
3. How to Spend Summer Holiday in China?		
4. On the Application of Mind-Mapping in English Academic Writing		
5. How did Deng Xiaoping Begin Chinese Economic Reform?		
6. Internet Negative Effects on People's Social Skills Today		
7. How to Develop Students' Critical Thinking Ability in Free Writing Teaching?		

(Continued)

Titles	Conceptual essay	Empirical essay
8. Empirical Study on Effects of Immersion Teaching Method in Second Language Classroom		
9. How to Live in City on 10 Yuan a Day		
10. On Effects of Overconsumption of Sugar on People's Body		

6 Self-Evaluation

(1) Look at the ways and principles of choosing a title again. Cross out any ideas you don't think necessary for your paper. Add more ideas if you want to.

(2) Complete this checklist to evaluate your own essay title. Does the final title have these things? Check (√) yes or (×)no.

1. Can the selected title for your research paper be valuable for research?		
2. Can the title of the research paper be scientific or revealing scientific laws?		
3. Does your final title have too many things to discuss?		
4. Is your final title very unique or innovative?		
5. Would you be interested in your research title?		
6. Is it difficult to find the needed sources or materials for your final topic?		
7. Are you very familiar with your selected title or topic?		
8. Had lots of people have discussed about your final title before?		
9. Do you have a logical structure to develop your final research paper about the title?		
10. Is your final title liked only by yourself?		

RESEARCH

Chapter 3

Source Research and Evaluation

In this chapter, you will:

√ Know types of information resources,

√ Evaluate reliable sources you need,

√ Identify the information you are looking for,

√ Know how to take notes of the selected sources.

1 Critical Thinking Questions

Directions: Work in small groups, or individually, or with a partner, to discuss the following open questions.

■ What kind of information do you look for in these places? Share your ideas with your partner and be as specific as you can.

public library	
university library	
dictionary	
books	
journals	
newspapers	
magazines	
official websites	
online	
WeChats	

■ What are the advantages or disadvantages of online sources?

■ What are the reasons why a person might do research in the library instead of online, or do research online instead of in the library?

② Types of Finding Information

Researching is a series of decisions about the content and literature review of the academic writing, with forms of note-taking or sketching or diagramming, which is a natural part of most people's academic writing process. It happens at all stages of the writing process, from first to last. Therefore, when you write, you need to find additional factual information to support and convince your writing. For beginning writers in the college, information sources usually are as follows: the local and online.

(1) Using the library

In modern university library or public library, you have access to most information needed in your research paper. Libraries provide awesome access to human ideas, knowledge and culture through books and periodicals. Newspapers is also one form to find information. Articles and stories published in newspapers are good facts to support academic writing development.

Usually, students in the college can search library information by using these techniques to find results:

a) Book indexes: search by author, title, subject and keywords.

b) Periodical indexes: find articles in specific journals or magazines by subject categories, title, author, keywords.

c) Newspaper indexes: find articles and stories published in sources of local, national and worldwide newspapers by subject categories, title, facts, keywords, etc.

(2) Searching information online

The most current information sources are likely to be found on the Internet. Most college students now use online searches to find information, which sometimes may lead them to physical university libraries, but a general online search is a good way to begin researching.

These days, popular online search websites or databases in China are CNKI http://www.cnki.net, Wanfang http://www.wanfangdata.com.cn, VIP http://www.cqvip.com or Baidu; from a global perspective, online search engines include Google http://www.google.com, and Ask http://www.ask.com.

As is known, begin to search online by using key words. These key words will identify your final topic and the specific information you are finding. You can search with several different search engines, to see if you can get different results. Exactly, websites are not more or less reliable than printed sources, so they may not be an authority in their field. Be careful to use them.

扩展阅读: 3.1

Library and Web Sources

Activity 1 »

Directions: Work with a partner. Imagine that you need to find the information on the following topics. Please try and compare different types of resources, and then share your ideas with your partner.

(1) The Effect of Role Model upon the Attitudes of Young Students

(2) Determinants of Classroom Psycho-social Environments

(3) High School Girls' Perceptions of Science and Its Impact on Their Career Choice

(4) A Symposium on the Catholic Ethic and Feminism

(5) The Effects of El Nino

(6) College Courses' Application Process

(7) Homeschooling in China

(8) Causes of American Civil War

3 Research Skills

Before you start looking for sources, you should consider what you already have, like your own ideas, lecture notes, textbooks, or recommended sources. Once you have got these, you can start your research. How to avoid wasting your time searching in the library or online, and how to help you find focused resources quickly, all of which involves your research skills. You will need to:

a) know what you are looking for when doing the research, having a research focus in mind,

b) be familiar with the necessary basic search tools,

c) identify reliable resources that cover the specific areas you need to write about,

d) search for resources of the specific questions your essay needs to address, not looking for every book or article related to a general topic,

e) search from general to particular, and read the useful sections of sources only, not reading all of them,

f) note down the full details of the resources for documentation by taking notes,

g) most importantly, know how to narrow the results.

For example, looking for sources about the title: *What Are Speed-Driving Initiatives in China between Countryside and Downtown*? The easy way is to use key words to narrow down search results in the library or online. The common ways to narrow the results are as follows:

Use these search ways to narrow the results:

- Use quotation marks to group words together:

    E.g. "speed-driving initiatives"

- Use "+" sign to ensure all key words included:

    E.g. "speed-driving initiatives" + China

- Use different forms of key words if necessary:

    E.g. "speed-driving initiatives" + Chinese/China

- Use "-"sign to exclude words you don't want:

    E.g. "speed-driving initiatives" + China - gender

- Use "OR" to search for two different word forms at the same time:

E.g. "speed-driving initiatives" + China +downtown OR countryside

- Change the order of key words for search:

  E.g. China +"speed-driving initiatives"

- Add more key words:

  E.g. "speed-driving initiatives" + China +downtown + countryside

扩展阅读: 3.2

Conducting Research

Activity 2 »

Directions: Work individually or in a small group. Find out the following information online by using research skills. What key words would you use to find information? Please compare your answer with your partner.

(1) Killing or being healthy about sports?

(2) Life on campus is interesting or monotonous?

(3) College students' everyday expenses

(4) The feudalistic thoughts of some young people today

(5) Qualifications for a good teacher

(6) On values of different generations concerning education of children

(7) Job discrimination against women in China

(8) Private schools should or should not be encouraged in China?

(9) Financial methods in competitive electricity markets

(10) Productivity growth and technical change in the generation of electricity.

4 Principles of Researching

Academic writing normally requires that you support your ideas and opinions with facts, statistics, quotations, and similar kinds of information. You get these kinds of supporting details from outside sources, such as books, journals, newspapers, websites, personal interviews. Thus, the search for relevant sources usually follows certain principles in order to collect information in a limited period of time.

(1) Focus on the theme, having a clear aim for data collection.

(2) Distinguish between facts and opinions. If you express an opinion, you must support it with facts.

(3) Select true, accurate and verifiable materials.

(4) Search typical, relevant and novel materials.

(5) If possible, do not quote second-hand literature. In academic papers, sources must always be quoted in the original.

(6) Preferably use up-to-date literature.

(7) Do not use any unserious sources, like popular newspapers, students' notes, course works, WeChat chatting, and so on.

Activity 3 »

Directions: Work with a partner. According to principles of researching, brainstorm and decide some specific pieces of information you need to research about the topic: *Comparison of Homeschooling between China and America.*

Theme	
Facts of China	
Facts of America	
Opinion in favor of **or** against homeschooling in China	
Opinion in favor of **or** against homeschooling in America	

5 Criteria of Source Evaluation

Source evaluation refers to the process of critically evaluating and judging the quality of selected sources. Data and Web evaluation have similar criteria but with a little difference.

Evaluation of Web sources:

Authorship: the author, editor or publisher of the document should be mentioned.

Publishing organization: the name, organizer, or reputation of organization should be recognized.

Target group: the purpose is to appeal to an academic target group, without advertisement or commercial information.

Precision: the document should not contain any mistakes, or imprecise references or out-of-date links.

Currency: the date of publication of the document should be included.

Permanence: it must not be possible to alter the document at will.

View objectivity: opinions in Web source should be objective. The strong or emotional language may indicate a bias.

Evaluation of data:

Structure: Glance at book's content or article's abstract to see if data is relevant to the theme.

Publication status: Mostly, publications will be authorized and well-received.

Purpose: Skim the title and first few paragraphs to examine its purpose.

Target audience: Look at intended audience of data according to its style, tone, dictation, or words.

Authorship: Judge the author's professional titles, research position, reputation and so on.

Activity 4 »

Directions: Work in small groups or with a partner. Look at the Web page below and evaluate it, according to criteria of source evaluation.

Name of sources: _____

Purpose of publishing organization: _____

Target group of this site: _____

Authorship: _____

Recently updated: _____

Objective or subjective views? _____

Mostly facts or opinions? _____

Any links? _____

Any advertisements? _____

Do you think it's a reliable source? Why or why not? _____

CHINADAILY.COM.CN | Q | Global Edition ASIA | 中文 双语 Français | Sign In | Subscribe

| HOME | CHINA | WORLD | BUSINESS | LIFESTYLE | CULTURE | TRAVEL | WATCHTHIS | SPORTS | OPINION | REGIONAL | FORUM | NEWSPAPER ▾ | MOBILE |

Business   Macro   Companies   Industries   Technology   Motoring   China Data   Finance   Top 10

• Home / Business / Industries

Report: Nation's mobile application market is thriving

By Ouyang Shijia | China Daily | Updated: 2020-04-14 08:57   f y in +

Passengers use mobile apps in a subway train in Beijing. [Photo by Feng Yongbin/China Daily]

Chinese mobile application market is thriving, and it has witnessed new growth opportunities amid the novel coronavirus outbreak, global business intelligence firm App Annie said in a new report.

Most Viewed in 24 Hours

Big data: How will Chinese spend Labor Day holiday amid COVID-19?

Rural couple wins hearts in videos with bucolic charm

Top 10 countries by patent applications

Top 10 world's richest people in 2020

Yuan's role in global payments increases

State Council News

Premier stresses processing proposals

Quick view: State Council executive meeting on April 28

Top 10

According to App Annie, 11 Chinese companies figured in its annual Top 52 Publishers list. Among the Chinese companies, nine are gaming app publishers.

Tencent Holdings Ltd, China's top gaming and social media operator, retained its top spot in App Annie's Top 52 Publishers list. Chinese leading gaming outfit NetEase was placed second in the ranking, followed by US-based gaming firm Activision Blizzard.

Chen Duan, executive director of the Zhongjing Digital Economy Research Center, said China's booming mobile application market is being driven by the country's huge user base.

"The future looks bright for gaming apps," Chen said. "As the restrictions on physical gathering continue amid the novel coronavirus pneumonia outbreak, those who find themselves stuck at home will spend more time on online games."

Due to the novel coronavirus outbreak, average mobile usage has risen by 30 percent to five hours a day in China from a year ago during February, the App Annie report said. Business and education apps were among the most widely used as many chose to work and study from home.

"With people spending more time indoors, they are turning to mobiles for entertainment," the report said.

"Apart from gaming, consumers also turned to social media and video streaming apps for entertainment and for keeping in touch with loved ones."

Other apps that saw strong growth in usage included food and grocery delivery apps, finance apps and medical and health and fitness apps.

"A growing number of consumers have experienced new digital services, and they will maintain the new consumption habits after the epidemic ends," Ouyang said. "It will also accelerate the digital transformation of traditional industries, which will help inject new impetus for the growth of the app market in China."

Top 10 countries by patent applications

Editor's picks

Over half of bankers consider monetary policy 'moderate'

Minimum wages in 6 regions lift above 2,000 yuan

China Data

A look at China's Q1 economic data

Q&A With CEO

Japanese consumer goods giant Kao to boost R&D, investment

Related Stories

Platforms help sell Hubei foodstuffs

Podcast apps make their voices heard

Local food-delivery services struggle as virus lifts demand

Audio books − popular, pleasurable

Self-driving vehicles set to become common

BACK TO THE TOP

HOME   CHINA   WORLD   BUSINESS   LIFESTYLE   CULTURE   TRAVEL   WATCHTHIS   SPORTS   OPINION   REGIONAL   FORUM   NEWSPAPER ▾   MOBILE

CHINADAILY.COM.CN 中国·报网

FOLLOW US

About China Daily

Advertise on Site

Contact Us

Job Offer

Expat Employment

6 Note-Taking for Selected Sources

Information in the libraries and online is numerous and up-dated quickly. Nobody has such a good memory to remember everything that he has read. Thus, it is necessary to take good notes for literature research.

It is more convenient to note down literatures by cards or specific software, like Notebook, Notefirst, etc. Here, the simple and easy way for students in the college is to take notes on cards or separate papers. For documentation and avoiding plagiarism, make sure what to take down.

- Any useful information or facts that support the topic, writing one fact or piece of information on each card.
- The complete working bibliography of sources consulted, including author, title, publisher, publication, date, issue volume and numbers, or page numbers.
- Notes from different key sources.
- The date when you access it or the retrieval websites.

Also, ensure to place only one note on a card and to write selective, useful and typical information on notecard.

Here is a notecard for your reference:

Bibliographical note   Brief heading of title

How Critical Is Critical Thinking?

Ryan D. Shaw, Music Educators Journal, Vol. 101, No. 2 (2014, 12), pp. 65-70

"Recent educational discourse is full of references to the value of critical thinking as a 21st-century skill. In education,   Main body critical thinking has been discussed in relation to problem   of notes solving, and some researchers suggest that training in critical thinking can improve students' responses to creativity."

08-05-2019

For opening quotes   Access date

Activity 5 »

Directions: Work individually to complete two specific note cards on the following topics you had searched. Then discuss and share your specific cards with your partner.

(1) Qualifications for a Good English Teacher

(2) On Values of Different Generations Concerning Education of Children

7 Put it Together

Directions: Review and write down the important points which are covered in this chapter.

(1) Types of finding information

| |
| |
| |
| |
| |
| |

(2) Research skills

| |
| |
| |
| |
| |
| |

(3) Principles of researching

| |
| |
| |
| |
| |
| |

(4) Criteria of source evaluation

| |
| |
| |
| |
| |
| |

Chapter 4
Developing an Outline

In this chapter, you will know:

√ Types of outlines,

√ Formats of outlines,

√ Parallelism in outlines,

√ Logical consistency in outlines.

 **Critical Thinking Questions**

Directions: Work in small groups and discuss the following open questions.

■ Why is it necessary to write an outline?

> Reasons for creating an outline

■ How do we write an outline? Write down some ways in the box.

> Ways of writing an outline

■ What are the components for an effective outline?

> Components for an effective outline

Introduction to Outline

An outline plays an important role in the process of writing a research essay. Specifically, it is your essay's map. In order to write a good essay, knowing the types of outlines is your first consideration.

扩展阅读: 4.1

What is an outline?

TYPES OF OUTLINES

Generally speaking, there are two kinds of outlines: *topic outline* and *sentence outline*. Which one you would like to choose, to a large extent, depends on your preference and that of your instructor.

- **Topic outline:** A topic outline includes words, phrases, or clauses, which means there are no complete sentences in it. The entries in a topic outline should have the same grammatical form or parallel structure. Suppose you choose to use a noun phrase as the first entry, then the following entries should follow this style by using noun phrases consistently. At the same time, you have to pay more attention to the grammatical form of entries, making your outline clear and logical.

- **Sentence outline:** Different from the topic outline, entries of a sentence outline are all complete sentences. If you like to use the sentence outline, then you have to follow the consistency and parallel rule, just like the topic outline. Meanwhile, being clear and logical is another thing you have to consider when you write a sentence outline.

FORMATS OF OUTLINES

The number-letter (alphanumeric) sequence and the decimal (十 进 位 的) pattern are the two basic formats for an outline. In terms of logic, both of the formats require at least two items for headings and subheadings.

The number-letter (alphanumeric) sequence is shown as follows:

Ⅰ. Introduction

Thesis: _____

Ⅱ. Body Paragraph 1

Topic Sentence: _____

A. Supporting idea

　1. First detail

　2. Second detail

B. Supporting idea

　1. First detail

　2. Second detail

III. Body Paragraph 2

　Topic Sentence: _____

　　......

　　......

VI. Conclusion

The sequence for a decimal outline（十进制提纲）proceeds as follows:

1. Introduction

　Thesis: _____

2. Body Paragraph 1

　Topic Sentence: _____

　2.1 Supporting idea

　　2.1.1 First detail

　　2.1.2 Second detail

　2.2 Supporting idea

　　2.2.1 First detail

　　2.2.2 Second detail

3. Body Paragraph 2

　Topic Sentence: _____

　　......

　　......

6. Conclusion

RULES OF OUTLINES

1) Parallelism: Entries or items, such as chapter titles, subtitles, or headings in one outline should be parallel. That's to say, entries at the same level of subordination should be grammatically organized in the same way. If you prefer to use a noun or noun phrase (such as

"Rapid development") as your first chapter title, then the following titles of each chapter should also be nouns or noun phrases.

2) Logical consistency: Parallelism requires outlines not only to be grammatical, but also to be logical. If an outline is not consistent in grammar, then it frequently signals problems in logic. Logical consistency means that headings and subheadings at each level of an outline are equally important and have similar categories of ideas. At the same time, each heading in an outline should demonstrate the same degree of generalization and carry approximately the similar information.

Activity 1 »

Directions: Work with a partner. Discuss and evaluate whether the entries of the following outlines are good or not. If not good, make necessary changes to make them more parallel and logical, according to what you've learned.

1. Ⅰ. Introduction to the Translation Project

    A. Background of Source Text

    B. Source Text's contents

    C. There are some reasons for Choosing the Text

  Ⅱ. To Analyze and Preparc Work of *Sociolinguistics* before Translation

    A. Text Analysis

    B. Stylistic Features and Translation Principles

    C. To design the Translation Process

2. Ⅰ. Canadian secondary schools during the nineteenth century

　Ⅱ. Changes in secondary school programs in Ontario from 1890 to 1930

　Ⅲ. Nature of secondary school curriculum changes from 1930 to 1970

　Ⅳ. Percentages of teenagers enrolled in high schools

3　Points to Consider in Developing an Outline

Have you ever thought of the reasons for writing an outline before you start to write an essay? Or what are the advantages of writing an outline? For one thing, outlines show what to write before you actually start writing. For another, outlines help to make your essay well organized and clearly focused. At last, outlines keep you from forgetting details.

Meanwhile, although readers won't see your outline, drawing up an outline in advance can be a useful way of organizing your ideas and seeing how they will work together. The following points have to be considered in developing an outline:

a. An outline starts with the thesis statement of an essay.

b. An outline demonstrates the essay's organization.

c. An outline tells what ideas you have to discuss first, second, third, (firstly, secondly, thirdly) and so on.

d. An outline ends with the conclusion of an essay.

Activity 2 »

Directions: Read the following sample outline. Answer the questions accordingly.

a. What will the thesis statement of the essay be?

b. How many paragraphs will there be in the main body?

c. How many supporting points will the third paragraph have? What will they be?

d. How many details will the fourth paragraph have? What will they be?

Don't Support Nuclear Energy

Ⅰ. Introduction

    A. Background information

    B. Thesis: Nuclear opponents citing dangers of nuclear power

Ⅱ. Nuclear power is very expensive

    A. Nuclear fuel is expensive

    B. Nuclear power stations are expensive to build and operate

        1. Cost of construction

        2. Cost of training workers

        3. Cost of safety features

Ⅲ. Nuclear materials are not safe

    A. Nuclear fuels are dangerous

        1. Mining fuels produce radioactive gas

        2. Working with radioactive fuels can harm workers

    B. Nuclear waste products are dangerous

        1. Nuclear waste is very radioactive

        2. Nuclear waste is difficult to dispose of or store safely

Ⅳ. A great possibility of accidents exists

    A. Nuclear power stations can fail

        1. Three Mile Island, USA (1979)

        2. Darlington, Canada (1992)

    B. Natural disasters can occur

        1. Earthquake: Kozloduy, Bulgaria (1977)

        2. Tornado: Moruroa, the Pacific (1981)

V. Conclusion

    A. Summarizing the points mentioned in text

    B. Suggestions: the world developing different types of energy to replace nuclear power

(*Source: extracted from Academic Writing from Paragraph to Essay, by Dorothy Zemach and Lisa Rumisek, p. 65*)

Possible Answers

a. _____

  _____

  _____

b. _____

  _____

  _____

c. _____

  _____

  _____

d. _____

  _____

  _____

4 How to Write an Outline

Before writing an outline, you have to carry out the usual process of gathering ideas, editing ideas, and deciding on a topic for your writing. In fact, writing an outline is a very useful and effective way of organizing your ideas logically and checking whether these ideas work together well or not.

Firstly, please number your ideas in order to demonstrate how these

扩展阅读: 4.2

How to develope
an outline?

ideas work together. With the purpose of avoiding confusion, try to use several types of numbers and letters to list your ideas. Remember to use Roman numbers (I, II, III, IV, V, VI, etc.) to introduce your essay's main idea of each part, such as introduction and the thesis statement, the main body paragraphs, and conclusion. The following framework is for you to turn to.

I. Introduction

II. First main idea

III. Second main idea

IV. Third main idea

V. Conclusion

Secondly, you have to fill in more detailed information for the paragraphs in the main body part by using capital Roman letters (A, B, C, etc.). One letter only stands for one supporting idea in the main body paragraph. An example is as follows:

I. Introduction

II. First main idea

    A. First supporting point

    B. Second supporting point

      ……

      ……

Finally, Arabic numerals (1, 2, 3, etc.) are used to give more details for the supporting ideas or points. Not every supporting idea or point has details. At the same time, some points may have several. Remember, sometimes it is not necessary to have the same number of details for every supporting point.

I. Introduction

II. First main idea

    A. First supporting point

      1. First detail

      2. Second detail

    B. Second supporting point

      1. First detail

      2. Second detail

      3. Third detail

      ……

      ……

By following aforementioned steps, you will have a general idea about how to write an outline.

Activity 3 »

Directions: Label each statement *T* for thesis statement, *M* for main idea, *S* for supporting point, or *C* for conclusion.

Title: The Advantages of Doing Yoga

a. _____ Cultivate quick and clear thinking.

b. _____ Physical advantages.

c. _____ Promote concentration.

d. _____ Relieve bad feelings.

e. _____ Mental advantages.

f. _____ Promote blood circulation.

g. _____ Promote digestion.

h. _____ Make you feel calm and peaceful.

i. _____ Cultivate self-confidence.

j. _____ Doing yoga regularly can be good for your body, your mind, and your emotions.

k. _____ Make you become flexible and healthy.

l. _____ So, you can build physical, mental, and emotional health by doing yoga.

m. _____ Emotional advantages.

Activity 4 »

Directions: Arrange the ideas in Activity 3 above into an outline; if possible, you may add the thesis statement and supporting ideas. Compare your finished outline with a partner.

Ⅰ. _____

Ⅱ. _____

    A. _____

    B. _____

Ⅲ. _____

    A. _____

    B. _____

    C. _____

Ⅳ. _____

A. _____

B. _____

C. _____

V. _____

Activity 5 »

Directions: Read the following essay, and complete the outline by filling in the missing parts. Then compare it with your partner's.

How to Succeed in a Job Interview

The competition on the job market is getting more and more intense. Just having a good school record and some certificates is not enough. Before getting a job, graduates from colleges must go through an interview with their potential employers. Generally, a job interview lasts from 30 to 40 minutes. As an applicant, you should demonstrate certain personal and professional qualities in the limited time available if you want to succeed in getting the desired position.

You should, for example, dress neatly and modestly. If you dress too informally, the interviewer may think that you are not serious about the interview or that you may be casual about your future work. Clothes that are too expensive or too colorful may suggest that you do not understand what behavior is appropriate for the job. It may not be true that "clothes make the man", but the first and often lasting impression of you is determined by the clothes you wear.

Besides caring for personal appearance, you should pay close attention to your manner of speaking. As we know, speech may show one's personality. For this reason, you should show your confidence by speaking in a clear voice, loud enough to be heard. Moreover, your speech must show you to be a friendly and pleasant person.

During the interview, you can talk about your own training, experience and other qualifications. The interviewer can determine whether your background and potential fit the position for which you are applying. Knowing something about the position helps you ask the right questions about the work and the requirements for the job. The interviewer can decide from your questions whether you are really interested or have the necessary knowledge or experience. It is important that you show your understanding of the requirements and your abilities for meeting these requirements.

Finally, to be really impressive, you must show confidence in yourself and enthusiasm for work. The manner you dress and speak helps, of course. But you can still show them by preparing yourself with the necessary information and working out some questions about the job. In addition, the way you enter the room, sit, look at the interviewer, and fill out application forms and other papers may show that you have sufficient confidence in yourself. As a result, the interviewer may feel your enthusiasm for work if he or she finds you are eager to discuss the job rather than the salary.

In a word, if you show good personal and professional qualities, with just a bit of good luck, you will certainly succeed in the job interview.

(*Source*: *extracted from An Integrated Skills Course, 2nd Edition, Book 2, p.152-153*)

How to Succeed in a Job Interview

Ⅰ. **Introduction**

Thesis statement: As an applicant, you should demonstrate certain personal and professional qualities in the limited time available if you want to succeed in getting the desired position.

Ⅱ. **Body paragraphs**

A. _____

   1. _____

     _____

   2. _____

     _____

   3. _____

     _____

B. _____

   1. _____

     _____

   2. _____

     _____

C. _____

   1. _____

   2. _____

   3. _____

D. _____

   1. _____

     _____

   2. _____

     _____

   3. _____

     _____

Ⅲ. **Conclusion**

Concluding sentence: If you show good personal and professional qualities, with just a bit of good luck, you will certainly succeed in the job interview.

Activity 6 »

Directions: Read the above essay *How to Succeed in a Job Interview* again, and then answer the following questions.

1. How many paragraphs does this essay contain? How many paragraphs are there in the body?

2. Do you think there are enough main ideas to develop the thesis statement? Do you think there are enough supporting points for each main idea? Give your reasons.

5 **How to Evaluate an Outline**

Before writing your essay, there are three issues you have to consider — to examine your outline for organizational structure, supporting points, and topic development. Here is an outline checklist.

Organizational structure

☐ Each paragraph is in the right order.
☐ The supporting points and details are in the right order.

Supporting points

☐ Every main idea is linked to the thesis statement.
☐ Every supporting point is linked to the paragraph's main idea.
☐ Each detail is linked to the paragraph's supporting points.

Topic development

☐ There are enough main ideas to develop the thesis statement.
☐ There are enough supporting points for each main idea.
☐ There are enough (and not too many) details for each supporting point.

Activity 7 »

Directions: Write a simple outline about your life. First, only outline the main body paragraphs. Your main ideas could include physical characteristics, your personality, your habits, your family, places you have lived, jobs you have had, things you like and dislike, and so on.

Effectively Evaluating Website Proposals

Activity 8 »

Directions: Explain your outline to a partner. Your partner will then add a thesis statement and a concluding sentence.

_____
_____
_____
_____
_____
_____
_____
_____
_____

Activity 9 »

Directions: Join another group and present your complete outline.

_____
_____
_____
_____
_____
_____
_____
_____
_____

6 Put it Together

Directions: Review and write down the important points which are covered in this chapter.

1. Types and formats of an outline.

_____

_____

_____

_____

_____

2. Points to consider when writing an outline.

_____

_____

_____

_____

_____

_____

3. The ways of writing an outline.

_____

_____

_____

_____

4. The ways of evaluating an outline.

_____

_____

_____

_____

_____

Chapter 5

Academic Language of Essay

In this chapter, you will know:

√ The definition of academic language,

√ Features of academic language,

√ Connecting words and signal words.

1 Critical Thinking Questions

Directions: Work in small groups or individually to finish the following task.

Do you think the following sentences are well chosen in words? If the words are improper, please explain the reason and rewrite.

1. When our car *died*, the *cops* were very *cool*; they called a tow truck, which got there *in a flash*.

    Well-chosen word: _____ (Yes)

    Reason: _____.

    Improper word: _____ (No)

    Rewrite: _____.

2. I was like really *freaked out* when I saw *the rents* dancing to rock music at my cousin's anniversary *bash*.

    Well-chosen word: _____ (Yes)

    Reason: _____.

    Improper word: _____ (No)

    Rewrite: _____.

3. Daniel was so *wiped out* after his workout at the gym that he couldn't *get it together* to defrost a frozen dinner.

    Well-chosen word: _____ (Yes)

    Reason: _____.

    Improper word: _____ (No)

    Rewrite: _____.

4. When Rick tried to *put the moves on* Lola at the school party, she told him to *shove off*.

    Well-chosen word: _____ (Yes)

    Reason: _____.

    Improper word: _____ (No)

    Rewrite: _____.

2 What is Academic Language?

The readability of an academic paper depends very much on its academic language presentation, so academic language in writing is in a special linguistic style.

Specifically speaking, academic language used in English writing must be formal, sober and factual, objective, clear and simple, accurate and precise, free of subjective judgments. As far as you state your opinions or points, the language must be clearly recognizable and explicit.

Actually, English is not only an international communicative language, but also one important international academic language. More and more scholars and researchers are paying much more attention to the importance of English demonstrated in sorts of international events and activities. With English as the target working language, these professionals are dedicating to constructing or making their specialty dissertations/papers published on relevant international journals/magazines, or attending international academic conferences, so English as one academic language is undoubtedly significant in the international academic status.

Overall, no matter what kind of academic papers, general academic papers or specific research papers, writing in English is aiming at delivering professional knowledge, reporting research findings and exploring academic problems, which results in the academic language used here being distinctive from common communicative language.

Activity 1 »

Directions: Work with your partner and discuss the following critical thinking questions. Then please share your ideas with other groups.

1. What are the distinctive features between general language and academic language?
2. Work in groups and list some examples of general language and academic language.

3 Features of Academic Language

There are altogether *five* foregrounding features showing in academic language, which can be without more difficulty in distinguishing from common communicative language.

> **1) Complexity:**
>
> Being complicated in structure, choosing terms and big words, extensively using notional/conceptual words or expressions and plenty of modifiers, etc.
>
> *For example:*
>
> 1. *Obviously the government is frightened of how the unions will react if it tries to make them behave properly.*
>
> 2. *Obviously the government is frightened of unions' reaction to its move to impose proper behavior on unions.* (*Academic language*)

扩展阅读: 5.1

Levels of Words

Activity 2 »

Directions: Work in pairs and explain which of the following sentences is better in using academic language according to the complexity of academic language's feature. Tell your reasons.

1. Researchers have suggested ways of making second language teaching and testing more "communicative" on the grounds that a communicative approach better reflects the nature of language proficiency than one which emphasizes the acquisition of discrete language skills (Canale and Swain, 1980; Oller, 1979b).

2. With economic specialization and the development of external economic linkages, division of labor intensifies, a merchant class is added to the political elite, and selective migration streams add to the social and ethnic complexities of cities.

3. This article analyses the constitutional aspects behind the formation of the first and second National Governments, examining in particular the role of the king in the formation of the two governments.

2) Formality:

Referring to using/applying the written English words, avoiding oral English words and abbreviated ones.

For example:

1. Oral English words: "stuff ", "a lot of", "thing", "sort of", ...

2. Abbreviated words: "can't", "doesn't", "shouldn't", ...

3. Simple expressions: "put off", "bring up", "make up", ...

4. Interrogative sentences: "What is it?", "How to do it?", "Is it right?", ...

Activity 3 »

Directions: Work in groups or pairs. Please use long and complex words to substitute the following vocabularies.

1. a lot of; plenty of   _____

2. more and more   _____

3. think   _____

4. so   _____

3) Objectivity:

Avoiding using first person pronouns — "I", "me", "my", "myself" etc., and second person pronoun "you"; extensively using third person pronouns, passive voice and objective expressions.

For example:

1. The data indicate that ...

2. This is where the disagreements and controversies begin ...

3. Several possibilities emerge ...

4. Of course, more concrete evidence is needed before ...

Activity 4 »

Directions: Work in pairs and discuss how to demonstrate the feature of objectivity in the following sentences, and then share your ideas in class.

1. From the above analysis, it can be inferred that …

2. The above analysis seems to indicate that the Internet plays a significant role in our daily life.

3. According to the above analysis …

4) Accuracy:

Referring to exactness in selecting words and citing statistics. The meaning of a word basically includes two aspects: denotative and connotative, which are contributing to a variety of words/expressions based on the same concept, while these word choices vary in moods and context. Thus, the exactness and delicacy are in option.

For example:

1. *"money", "cash", "currency", "capital", "funds";*

2. *Specific choices in date, data, citation, etc.; and avoiding using many years ago or a lot of people, etc.*

Activity 5 »

Directions: Work in pairs and analyze the following English translations according to the accuracy feature of academic language.

1. 我们对词汇教学越来越有兴趣。

(1) We're more and more interested in vocabulary teaching.

(2) We've more and more interests in vocabulary teaching.

_____.

(3) We are increasingly interested in vocabulary teaching.

(4) There are growing interests in vocabulary teaching.

_____.

(5) Vocabulary teaching has attracted increasing interests.

(6) Increasing interests have been directed to vocabulary teaching.

_____.

2. 人们对词汇学习做了很多研究。

(1) We've done a lot of research about vocabulary learning.

_____.

(2) There is much research about vocabulary learning.

_____.

(3) Much research has been done about vocabulary learning.

_____.

(4) Considerable research has been conducted regarding vocabulary learning.

_____.

5) Ambiguity:

Referring to the appropriate use of ambiguity in expressing standpoint and viewpoint to some degree, avoid absolute opinions and obey facts, showing tentative statements.

For example:

1. *Modal verbs: will, would, may, might, could;*

2. *Frequency adverbs: often, sometimes, and usually;*

3. *Modal adverbs: definitely, clearly, probably, possibly, perhaps;*

4. *Probability verbs: seem, look like, tend to, believe, suggest, assume, and indicate;*

5. *Probability nouns: assumption, possibility, probability.*

In conclusion, in control of these features of academic language, the scholars and researchers are capable to write out good research reports, thesis and monographs, meeting the criterion to norm. Extremely important, when any thoughts or writings of another person are used, the sources must be clearly identified (using quotes, bibliography and giving reference), which will be mentioned in Chapter 7 and 9.

Activity 6 ≫

Directions: Work in pairs and discuss how to make tentative statements? Please give examples to illustrate.

Modals	Verbs	Adverbs	Adjectives	Assumption nouns

Activity 7 »

Directions: Work with your partner and discuss the following critical thinking question.

What should you pay serious attention to when you are preparing and crafting your academic essays, making reference to other professional journals on the internet or scholarly papers in magazines?

_____

_____

_____

_____

_____

_____

4 Connecting Words and Signal Words in Writing

Coherence is one of the most important factors in displaying the effectiveness of academic writings, which counts in two aspects respectively: sentence writing and paragraph writing.

For sentence writing, a sentence is coherent when its words or parts are properly connected and their relationships are unmistakably clear. Here sentence coherence mostly focuses on connective words: coordinating and

扩展阅读: 5.2

Effective Sentences

subordinating conjunctions.

For paragraph writing, coherence may not be perfect even if the sentence is written skillfully and is arranged in a clear, logical order. Therefore, good transitions should be used/ employed so that one sentence runs smoothly to another to make an effective paragraph or a whole academic essay.

1) Coordinating conjunctions

Coordinating conjunctions connect grammatically equal elements. Coordinating conjunctions are sometimes called the "Fan Boys" conjunctions—such as *for, and, nor, but, or, yet, and so*. For details, see Table 1.

(*Extract from Alice Oshima; Ann Hogue: 190, Appendix D*)

Table 1

Conjunction	Function	Example
for	Connecting a reason to a result	I am a little hungry, *for* I didn't eat breakfast this morning.
and	Connecting equal or similar ideas	John likes to fish *and* hunt.
nor	Connecting two negative sentences	She doesn't eat meat, *nor* does she drink milk.
but	Connecting different equal ideas	I like to eat fish *but* not to catch them.
or	Connecting two equal choices	Do you prefer coffee *or* tea?
yet	Connecting equal contrasting ideas	It is sunny *yet* cold.
so	Connecting a result to a reason	I did not eat breakfast this morning, so I am a little hungry.

Conjunction Pairs	Function	Example
both…and	Connecting equal or similar ideas	Both San Francisco and Sydney have beautiful harbors.
not only…but also	Connecting progressive ideas	Japanese food is not only delicious to eat but also beautiful to look at.
either…or	Connecting two equal choices	Bring either a raincoat or an umbrella when you visit Seattle.
neither…nor	Connecting two equal negative choices	My grandfather could neither read nor write, but he was a very wise person.
whether…or	Connecting two equal choices	The newlyweds could not decide whether to live with her parents or to rent an apartment.

Activity 8 »

Directions: For each set of sentences, please connect them to make a compound sentence or a simple sentence with coordinating conjunctions you have learned.

1. It became very dark. Mark was suddenly frightened.

_____

2. He heard a noise. He decided to go back to his own room.

_____

3. The little girl walked for a long time. She couldn't find the road.

_____.

4. Finally, Bob became very tired. He tried to have a rest. He had to struggle with his fear to go to sleep.

_____.

5. The little kid cried for help. No one heard her.

_____.

6. There are twenty students in the room. Yang alone can do the work.

_____.

7. He is a good pianist. He is also a good singer.

_____.

8. We have made some progress. We still have a long way to go.

_____.

9. The new workers are young and inexperienced. They are eager to learn from the veteran workers.

_____.

10. The sky was cloudless. The sun was shining brightly.

_____.

2) Subordinating conjunctions

Subordinating conjunctions apparently appear in the position of subordinating clause or clauses to show its or their relation(s) with the main clause(s). See Table 2.

(*Extract from Alice Oshima; Ann Hogue*: 190-191, *Appendix D*)

Table 2

Time (When?)	
after	After we ate lunch, we decided to go shopping.
as, just as	Just as we left the house, it started to rain.
as long as	We waited as long as we could.
as soon as	As soon as the front door closed, I looked for my house key.
before	I thought I had put it in my coat pocket before we left.
since	I have not locked myself out of the house since I was 10 years old.
until	Until I was almost 12, my mother pinned the key to my coat.
when	When I turned 12, my mother let me keep the key in my pocket.
whenever	I usually put the key in the same place whenever I come home.
while	While I searched for the key, it rained harder and harder.
Place (Where?)	
where	I like to shop where prices are low.
wherever	I try to shop wherever there is a sale.
anywhere	You can find bargains anywhere you shop.
everywhere	I use my credit card everywhere I shop.
Manner (How?)	
as, just as	I love to get flowers as most women do.
as if	You look as if you didn't sleep at all.
as though	She acts as though she doesn't know us.
Distance (How far? How near? How close?)	
as + adverb + as	We will hike as far as we can before it turns dark.
	The child sat as close as she could to her mother.
	The child sat as close to her mother as she could.
Frequency (How often?)	
as often as	I call my parents as often as I can.
Reason (Why?)	
as	I can't take evening classes, as I work at night.
because	I can't take evening classes because I work at night.
since	I can't take evening classes since I work at night.

(Continued)

Purpose (For what purpose?)	
so that	Many people emigrate so that their children can have a better life.
in order that	Many people emigrate in order that their children can have a better life.

Result (With what result?)	
so + adjective + that	I was so tired last night that I fell asleep at dinner.
so + adverb + that	She talks so softly that the other students cannot hear her.
such a(n) + noun + that	It was such an easy test that most of the students got A.
so much/many/ little/ few + noun + that	He is taking so many classes that he has no time to sleep.

Condition (Under what condition?)	
if	We will not go hiking if it rains.
unless	We will not go hiking unless the weather is perfect.

Concession contrast	
although,even though, though	I love my brother although/even though/though we disagree about almost everything.

Contrast (Direct opposites)	
while	My brother likes classical music, while I prefer hard rock.
whereas	He dresses conservatively, whereas I like to be a little shocking.

To refer to people	
who, whom, whose, that (informal)	People who live in glass houses should not throw stones.
	My parents did not approve of the man whom my sister married.
	An orphan is a child whose parents are dead.

To refer to animals and things	
which	My new computer, which I bought yesterday, stopped working today.
that	Yesterday I received an e-mail that I did not understand.

To refer to a time or a place	
when	Thanks giving is a time when families travel great distances to be together.
where	An orphanage is a place where orphans live.

That clauses	
that	Do you believe that there is life in outer space?
	I think that the bus is coming soon.

(Continued)

If/Whether clauses	
whether	I can't remember whether I locked the door.
whether or not	I can't remember whether or not I locked the door.
whether… or not	I can't remember whether I locked the door or not.
if	I can't remember if I locked the door.
Question clauses	
who, whoever, whom, which, what, where, when, why, how, how much, how many, how long, how often, etc.	Whoever arrives at the bus station first should buy the tickets.
	Do you know where the bus station is?
	We should ask when the bus arrives.
	He didn't care how long he had to wait.
	Do not worry about how much they cost.
	…

Activity 9 »

Directions: Rewrite the following paragraph with the subordinating conjunctions you have learned.

I got up a little later than usual on Sunday morning. I washed and had a quick breakfast. I started going to town to buy the dictionary recommended by the teacher. At the school gate I saw Li Ping. I asked him if he was going to town too, and he said that he was. So we decided to go together. All the buses were crowded. We had to wait for a long time at the bus stop before we could get on a bus. An hour later we got off the bus at a busy street. There were three bookstores there. We went to the first one and didn't find the dictionary. Then we went to the second one and the shop assistant said that the dictionary was sold out. I finally bought the dictionary at the third bookstore. After that Li Ping and I went to other stores and bought various things. We returned to school just in time for lunch.

3) Transitional signals

Transitional signals show the direction of a writer's thoughts. They are like the road signs that guide travelers. Please see more details, in Table 3.

(*Extract from Alice Oshima; Ann Hogue: 192-193, Appendix E*)

Transitional words or phrases make one sentence run smoothly to another; what's more, they not only help the paragraph develop as a fluent one, but also make the whole essay organized as a natural one.

There are many ways to develop a fluent and coherent paragraph and a natural essay. The effective ways are as follows:

- Using prepositional words and phrases.
- Using adverbs and conjunctions.
- Using transitional expressions.
- Using parallel structure.
- Repeating words or word groups.
- Using pronouns to refer to nouns in preceding sentences.
- Being consistent in the person and number of nouns and pronouns, and the tense of verbs.

Table 3

To list ideas in order of time	first, first of all, second, third, next, then, after that, meanwhile, in the meantime, finally, last, last of all, subsequently ...
To list ideas in order of importance	first, first of all, first and foremost, second, more important, most important, more significantly, most significantly, above all, most of all ...
To add similar or equal idea	also, besides, furthermore, in addition, moreover, too, as well...
To add an opposite idea	however, on the other hand, nevertheless, nonetheless, still ...
To explain or restate an idea	in other words, in particular, (more) specifically, that is ...
To make a stronger statement	indeed, in fact...
To give another possibility	alternatively, on the other hand, otherwise ...
To give an example	for example, for instance ...
To express an opinion	according to, in my opinion, in my view ...
To give a reason	for, because, since, as, because of ...
To give a result	accordingly, as a consequence, as a result, consequently, for these reasons, hence, therefore, thus ...
To add a conclusion	all in all, in brief, in short, to conclude, to summarize, in conclusion, in summary, for these reasons ...
To show similarities	likewise, similarly, also...
To show differences	however, in contrast, instead, on the contrary, on the other hand, rather ...

Activity 10 »

Directions: Read the following passage and pay attention to the use of cohesive conjunctions and transitional signals.

How Empathy Unfolds

The moment Hope, just nine months old, saw another baby fall, tears welled up in her own eyes and she crawled off to be comforted by her mother, as though it were she who had been hurt. And 15-month-old Michael went to get his own teddy bear for his crying friend Paul; when Paul kept crying, Michael retrieved Paul's security blanket for him. Both these small acts of sympathy and caring were observed by mothers trained to record such incidents of empathy in action. The results of the study suggest that the roots of empathy can be traced to infancy. Virtually from the day they are born infants are upset when they hear another infant crying – a response some see as the earliest precursor of empathy.

Developmental psychologists have found that infants feel sympathetic distress even before they fully realize that they exist apart from other people. Even a few months after birth, infants react to a disturbance in those around them as though it were their own, crying when they see another child's tears. By one year or so, they start to realize the misery is not their own but someone else's, though they still seem confused over what to do about it. In a research by Martin L. Hoffman at New York University, for example, a one-year-old brought his own mother over to comfort a crying friend, ignoring the friend's mother, who was also in the room.

Such motor mimicry, as it is called, is the original technical sense of the word empathy as it was first used in the 1920s by E. B. Titchener, an American psychologist. Titchener's theory was that empathy stemmed from a sort of physical imitation of the distress of another, which then evokes the same feelings in oneself. He sought a word that would be distinct from sympathy, which can be felt for the general plight of another with no sharing whatever that other person is feeling.

Motor mimicry fades from toddlers' repertoire at around two and a half years, at which point they realize that someone else's pain is different from their own, and are better able to comfort them. A typical incident, from a mother's diary:

A neighbor's baby cries and Jenny approaches and tries to give him some cookies. She follows him around and begins to whimper to herself. She then tries to stroke his hair, but he pulls away. He calms down, but Jenny still looks worried. She continues to bring him toys and to pat his head and shoulders.

At this point in their development toddlers begin to diverge from one another in their overall sensitivity to other people's emotional upsets, with some, like Jenny, keenly aware and others tuning out. A series of studies by Marian Radke-Yarrow and Carolyn Zahn-Waxler at the National Institute of Mental Health showed that a large part of this difference in empathic concern had to do with how parents disciplined their children. Children, they found, were more empathic when the discipline included calling strong attention to the distress their misbehavior caused someone else: "Look how sad you've made her feel" instead of "That was naughty". They found that children's empathy is also shaped by seeing how others react when someone else is distressed; by imitating what they see, children develop a repertoire of empathic response, especially in helping other people who are distressed. (Simon Greennall; Wen Qiufang: 29-30, 2016)

Discuss in small groups and identify:

1. Two types of conjunctions in this essay. (Inner-sentence)
2. Other conjunctive adverbs and transitional phrases inside sentence. (Inner-sentence)
3. Transitions among sentences and paragraphs.
4. Other connecting words among sentences and paragraphs.

Works cited: »

1. Alice Oshima; Ann Hogue. *Introduction to Academic Writing*, Third Edition, Pearson Education, Inc., 2007.

2. Simon Greenall; Wen Qiufang. *New Standard College English: An Integrated Course*, Second Edition, Foreign Language Teaching and Research Press, 2016.

5 Self-Evaluation

For each statement below, circle the word which is true for you.

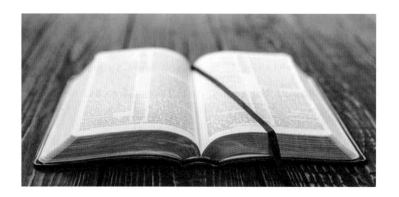

1. I understand what academic language is.	Agree	Disagree	Not sure
2. I know the features of academic language.	Agree	Disagree	Not sure
3. I know the differences between common language and academic language.	Agree	Disagree	Not sure
4. I know 5 typical features of academic language.	Agree	Disagree	Not sure
5. I know we should pay serious attention to plagiarism when writing academic writing.	Agree	Disagree	Not sure
6. I can find coordinating conjunctions very useful in sentence writing.	Agree	Disagree	Not sure
7. I can find subordinating conjunctions very useful in sentence writing.	Agree	Disagree	Not sure
8. I can find transition signals very useful both in paragraph writing and essay writing.	Agree	Disagree	Not sure
9. I know how to achieve coherence in academic writing.	Agree	Disagree	Not sure
10. I understand what effective writing is.	Agree	Disagree	Not sure

Chapter 6

Introduction, Conclusion and Peer Review

In this chapter, you will:

√ Learn how to write the introductory part,

√ Learn how to write the conclusion part,

√ Learn to review papers with a classmate effectively,

√ Make revision decisions.

① Critical Thinking Questions

Directions: Work in small groups and discuss the following open questions.

■ Do you think the introduction part is very important to a well-organized research essay? Why or why not?

■ If you want to deeply impress readers, you have to use specific language to signal your conclusion. Would you like to list some of these concluding signal words or phrases?

■ Do you think it is useful/necessary to have your classmates read your paper before your instructor does? Why or why not?

② The Introductory Part

If you want to write a well-organized research essay, there are three things you need to consider: how to write a good title, a strong introduction, and an effective conclusion.

An introductory part/paragraph usually includes two main points: **general statements** and the **thesis statement**. General statements are used to arouse the readers' interest, while the main idea of the essay is always stated by the thesis statement(More information about thes is studment can be shown in Chapter 8). Generally, from the introduction, readers may know the tone of the author, as well as the author's stance. It also shows the way the essay is organized. What roles does the introduction play in the research essay?

扩展阅读: 6.1

Introduction

Functions or roles of the Introduction

A well-written introductory part/paragraph usually plays the following important roles:

1. Arouse readers' interest and encourage them to continue reading the essay.

2. Provide the necessary background information. Readers may understand the research essay well under the guidance of background information.

3. Demonstrate a thesis statement. Usually, this statement of the main idea in the essay is put forward near the end of the introduction.

4. Present a plan of development of the essay.

In the introduction part, the writer always lists the major supporting points for the thesis orderly in which they will be presented. In some cases, the thesis and plan of development appear in the same sentence. However, writers sometimes choose not to describe the plan of development.

In short, the components of the introduction part usually embrace as follows:

1. Hook

2. Background information

3. Plan of essay development

4. Thesis statement

In fact, the components of hook and thesis statement are most important and essential.

(Source: extracted from College Writing Skills, eighth edition, by John Langan, 2011.)

Activity 1 »

Directions: Read each of the following sets of sentences. Put them in the correct order to form effective introductory paragraphs.

Paragraph 1

1. They are mostly born in the 70s or 80s and live in one of China's big cities.

2. They have a lot of money, but do not fall slave to it.

3. Their life may go something like this: turn off the mobile phone after work, eat only healthy food, meet friends every weekend, and like to help poor people.

4. You must have heard of white-collar and blue-collar workers, and possibly gold-collar workers as well.

5. In Beijing, the Green Collar Club is for people who want to "be happy, healthy and helpful".

6. A typical green collar is well educated like a white collar but physically strong like a blue collar.

7. They not only succeed in their careers, but also like to enjoy life.

8. Green collars even have their own club.

9. Recently, a new color of collar is making its way into China. It's green.

The right order of the introduction _____

Paragraph 2

1. An American host or hostess will usually offer food and drink only once.

2. If the food served is something you are unfamiliar with, you could ask for just a little.

3. For example, you could say "I'm not accustomed to eating such things."

4. During a meal, Americans show their hospitality differently from Chinese.

5. If you want something to eat or drink, you should accept it at the first time it is offered.

6. Do not refuse it, expecting that the host or hostess will make a second offer or insist on serving the food or drink.

7. Frequently guests are expected to help themselves to food and it is polite to finish all food on your plate.

8. If you don't like it, you should be honest and polite.

The right order of the introduction _____

Five common hooks of the introduction

Generally, there are five common methods (common hooks) of the introduction. When you write an essay, it's OK to use any of them, or combine some of them, in order to introduce your subject to the reader.

- **From a broad, general statement of your topic to a narrow, concrete thesis statement (From general idea to specific idea).** Narrowing down the broad, general statement makes the reader know exactly about your thesis statement after reading the introductory paragraph.

- **With an idea or a situation that is opposite to the one you are going to talk about.** The sharp contrast between the opening idea and the thesis that follows it makes the reader feel surprised, or even intrigued, which can invite and entice them to continue reading.

- **A brief story or an anecdote.** Stories or anecdotes in the introduction are interesting and impressive in itself. They may grab the reader's attention or arouse their curiosity immediately. Please note that the story or anecdote must be closely related to your main idea.

- **One or more questions.** By means of asking questions, you may either want the reader to consider the questions, or you may plan to answer the questions yourself later in the research essay.

- **A quotation.** A quotation can be what you have read in a book, an article or newspaper. A quotation can also be what you have heard, a well known saying or proverb, a current or recent slogan of an advertisement, or a favorite expression used by your friends or family members.

Activity 2 »

Directions: Read the following introduction parts and write down what kind of introduction method has been used in each case according to the above information of *Five common hooks of the introduction*.

Five common hooks of the introduction:

A. General to narrow

B. Starting with an opposite

C. Incident or story

D. Questions

E. Quotation

_____ 1. To many people, the answer to the question "What exactly is language for?" seems obvious. It's for the transfer of useful facts. The belief that "information talking" is primary role of language dates back at least to the 17th century, when the English philosopher John Locke argued in his influential *An Essay Concerning Human Understanding* (1690) that language is "the great conduit, whereby men convey their discoveries, reasoning, and knowledge to each other."

_____ 2. Early Sunday morning, the young mother dressed her little girl warmly and gave her a candy bar, a picture book, and a well-worn stuffed rabbit. Together, they drove down to a Methodist Church. There the mother told the little girl to wait on the stone steps until children began arriving for Sunday school. Then the young mother drove off, abandoning her five-year-old girl because she couldn't cope with being a parent anymore. This incident is one of thousands of cases of child neglect and abuse that occur annually. Perhaps the automatic right to become a parent should no longer exist. Would-be parents should be forced to apply for parental licenses for which they would have to meet three important conditions.

_____ 3. What is love? How do we know that we are really in love? When we meet that special person, how can we tell that the feelings are genuine and not merely infatuation? And, if they are genuine, will these feelings last? Love, as we all know, is difficult to define. But most people agree that true and lasting love involves far more than mere physical attraction. Love involves mutual respect, the desire to give rather than take, and the feeling of being wholly at ease.

_____ 4. When I decided to return to school at age thirty-five, I wasn't at all worried about my ability to do the work. After all, I was a grown woman who had raised a family, not a confused teenager fresh out of high school. But when I started classes, I realized that those "confused teenagers" sitting around me were in much better shape for college than I was. They still had all their classroom skills in bright, shiny condition, while mine had grown rusty from disuse. I had to learn how to locate information in a library, how to write a report, and even how to speak up in class discussions.

_____ 5. Moving to a new country can be an exciting experience. In a new environment, you somehow feel more alive. Seeing new sights, eating new food, and hearing the foreign sounds of a new language. Soon, however, this sensory bombardment becomes sensory overload. Suddenly, new experiences seem stressful rather than stimulating, and delight turns into discomfort. This is known as culture shock. Culture shock is more than jet lag or homesickness, and it affects nearly everyone who enters a new culture. Although not everyone experiences culture shock in exactly the same way, many experts agree that it has roughly five stages.

3 The Concluding Part

A concluding paragraph is your chance to remind the readers of your thesis idea and provide them with a natural and graceful end. As the final part in an essay, the conclusion has three purposes.

扩展阅读: 6.2

Conclusion

Three purposes of the final part:

Firstly, the conclusion signals the end of the essay, so you have to start your conclusion with a transition.

Secondly, the conclusion reminds the reader of your main points, so you have to either sum up your subtopics or paraphrase your thesis.

Finally, the conclusion impresses the reader with your final thought on the topic. Therefore, you should present a strong and effective message that makes your reader remember.

Techniques for writing conclusion:

Here are some techniques for you to follow in order to write an effective and strong conclusion.

1) End with a prediction.

Like questions, predictions may also involve the readers. A prediction demonstrates what will happen in the future.

For example:

Nowadays, people have known how the costs of going to college have been increasing, while, at the same time, sources of financial aid for students have been decreasing. If this tendency goes on, fewer and fewer parents will be willing to send their children to go to college.

2) End with a summary and final thought.

After presenting your thesis and supporting it, you have to restate the thesis and supporting points. But remember, avoid the exact wording you used before.

For example:

To sum up, online shopping has several advantages. Such shopping is quite easy and convenient, and saves your money and time as well. It's not surprising that more and more people are doing shopping on the Internet, for everything from clothes to household appliances.

3) End with a solution, make a recommendation, or call for action.

Both solutions and recommendations suggest what should be done about a problem or situation. Calling for action means you would like to persuade the reader to take specific steps to overcome the difficult problems or situations.

For example:

If people stop to think twice before they raise pets, there will be fewer cruelty to animals. To be specific, it's humans who adopt pets without thinking about the expense and responsibility involved, and then they abuse and neglect their pet animals. Now, it's time for people to stop the cruelty to animals and treat them kindly and affectionately, because they are living creatures too, not stuffed toys.

4) End with an authoritative quotation on the topic.

An authoritative quotation is a common method to conclude the essay, which may convince the readers and make a deep impression on them.

For example:

To conclude, with the rising costs and the declining financial aid, many people can't afford to go to college any longer. Now, it's essential and imperative for the government to increase funding for higher education. As Horace Mann argued in his **Fifth Annual Report***, a nation's economic wealth will increase through an educated public.*

Activity 3 »

Directions: Read the following *skeleton essays*. Only the introductory paragraph and topic sentences for the body paragraphs are given. Write a concluding paragraph for each essay.

Essay 1

Taking a Job Interview

Introductory Paragraph

A job interview can often make or break your chances of getting your dream job. There are several things that you can do in an interview to increase the possibility of your success.

Topic Sentences for Body Paragraphs

A. Dressing properly

B. Answering interview questions thoroughly

C. Asking good questions at the end of interview

Concluding Paragraph

_____

_____

_____

_____

_____

_____

_____

_____

_____

_____

_____

Essay 2

Studying in Great Britain

Introductory Paragraph

People come from all over the world to the United Kingdom to pursue education. Some come for a year, while others may stay four years or longer to complete a program or earn a degree. Of course, the first few weeks in a new country are always a little stressful, but knowledge of a few British characteristics and customs can smooth the path for new arrivals.

Topic Sentences for Body Paragraphs

A. British people are usually reserved.

B. British people are very orderly, so waiting in a queue for a bus or in a shop is a must.

C. The weather is no joke—it rains a lot.

D. Cars drive on the left side of the road, and stepping off a curb can be dangerous if you are not used to looking to the right instead of to the left.

Concluding Paragraph

_____

_____

_____

_____

_____

_____

_____

_____

_____

_____

_____

_____

4 Peer Review

In the university, **a peer** means your classmate who has been assigned the same task as you. Generally, in academic writing classes, teachers often ask students to exchange their papers and give comments on their classmates' writing. This is **peer review**.

扩展阅读: 6.3

Peer Review

But what is the purpose of peer review? In effect, peer review helps to solve two important questions: On one hand, peer review tells you how well a reader understands what you have written. On the other hand, peer review tells you how other people deal with the same assignment or task.

The first question: It is important because you don't know who your readers are and whether they can understand your ideas or not. While a peer reviewer plays the role of a reader, he or she will give you reasonable and objective suggestions from his or her perspective. What's more, he or she will not judge your ability or give you a grade. So, peer review is very valuable.

The second question: It is even more important. Reviewing other peers' essays provides you chances to study exactly the type of essay that you are writing as well. You have a chance to see how someone else like you meet the same challenges, such as how to present the thesis statement, how to write the strong introduction and conclusion, and whether the supporting ideas are effective. In a word, you may learn from others' strong points to offset your own weakness, and improve your future essay writing.

The followings are the points you have to remember:

For one thing, don't search for specific things when you review your peer's paper. Try to identify the thesis statement, topic sentences, and methods of support. Underline any parts of the writing that you don't understand. At last, point out what the writer does well. It's unnecessary to worry about the spelling and grammar mistakes, just focusing on its content, organization, and ideas.

For another, don't speak too many negative words, and be kind. There is no denying that it is difficult to share work with others, even though they do not assign you any grades.

When you do reviewing job, try to give response from a reader's perspective; that is, saying "I didn't understand this argument" rather than "You didn't argue this very clearly", and "Good conclusion" doesn't make any sense, so give reasons for your review or comment.

(*Source: extracted from Writing Research Papers by Dorothy E. Zemach & Daniel Broudy, et al., 2015.*)

Effective peer review worksheet:
1. Do the first few sentences of the introduction lead you to the thesis statement? Yes or No? Where is the thesis statement?
2. How many paragraphs are there in the body? What are the topics of the body paragraphs?
3. What kind of supporting details does the writer use in each body paragraph (examples, statistics, facts, etc.)?
4. Check each paragraph for unity. Is any sentence unnecessary or off the topic? Yes or No?
5. Check each paragraph for coherence. Does each one follow smoothly from beginning to the end? Yes or No? a. What key nouns are repeated? b. What transition signals can you find?
6. What expressions does the writer use to link paragraphs? If there is none, write none. (If there are more or fewer paragraphs, add or delete lines.) To introduce the first body paragraph: Between Paragraph 2 and 3: Between Paragraph 3 and 4:

Effective peer review worksheet:
Between Paragraph 4 and 5: To introduce the conclusion:
7. What kind of conclusion does this essay have — a summary of the main points or a statement of the thesis statement? Does the writer make a final comment? What is it? Is this an effective ending (one that you will remember)?
8. In your opinion, what is the best feature of this essay? In other words, what is this writer's best writing skill?

(*Source: Extracted from Peer-Editing Working sheet by Alice Oshima & Ann Hogue, 2011, p. 214.*)

Activity 4 »

Directions: Read these sentences from a peer reviewer's comments. Check (√) the ones that are useful and effective. Then discuss with a partner why the ones you didn't check are not useful or effective.

_____ Your essay is better because it has one more paragraph than mine.

_____ Your introduction shocks me, because I never know Americans eat so much sugar.

_____ I think your thesis statement is *Sugar poses a threat to the world's health*. However, it is the first sentence in the introduction and not the last one, so I'm not sure.

_____ Sugar is not a problem at all. I eat a lot of sugar, and I am healthy.

_____ Why is your essay so short?

_____ You say that sugar causes "a lot of health problems". Can you say what those health problems are?

_____ I like the comparison of eating sugar and a car needing fuel. That helps me understand the issue.

_____ I don't know if consuming sugar is the same as a car needing fuel. It's an interesting comparison, but are the two really the same?

_____ Your information about headaches in the conclusion should come earlier, in one of the body paragraphs. It's another health condition, so maybe in paragraph 4.

_____ I am sure that you will get an A on this essay.

_____ Your grammar is pretty bad. Please check and correct it.

NOTE:

After you and your classmate have reviewed research papers each other, meet in person and discuss the papers with each other. If your classmate makes any comments that you don't understand, ask for clarification. Answer any questions that are asked. Then it is time to decide how to revise your paper. Remember that suggestions from a peer reviewer are just that: *suggestions*. They are not orders. You are the writer, and make your own decision. At last, mark the changes that you want to make in your essay. Ask for any necessary help with grammar or vocabulary. Then you are ready to write your second draft.

Activity 5 »

Directions: Write an essay with the title "My Hobbies and Interests". You should write less than 250 words. After your first draft, exchange it with your partner and do peer review. Then discuss these questions.

Peer review form: essay

Your name: _____

Classmate's name: _____

Title of classmate's essay: _____

Date: _____

1. What is the topic?

_____

2. What's the thesis statement?

_____

_____

3. How many body paragraphs are there?

_____

_____

4. Does the introduction have a hook? What other information is in the introduction?

_____

5. Underline the topic sentence in each body paragraph. If you can't find one, note it here:

_____

_____

6. Write the number of each body paragraph and then explain what types of support are used for each paragraph. (Such as, quotations, logical reasoning, a comparison/ contrast, statistics, common knowledge, personal knowledge, examples.)

_____

_____

_____

_____

7. Does the conclusion tie back to the introduction? What functions does the conclusion fulfill?

_____

_____

8. Any other comments:

_____

_____

_____

9. After finishing, do you agree with the comment from the peer reviewer?

_____

_____

_____

_____

5 Put it Together

Directions: There are several important points covered in this chapter. Please review to write down them according to your understanding.

Mains points of this Unit:

1. An essay has three main parts, and they are

_____

_____

_____

2. The introductory part consists of two things, and they are

_____

_____

_____

3. The concluding paragraph reminds your reader of what you have said. In it, you should

_____

_____

_____

_____

4. The ways of peer review include

_____

_____

_____

_____

Chapter
In-Text Citation
7

In this chapter, you will:

√ Learn about in-text citation vs. plagiarism,

√ Learn about the principles and ways of in-text citation,

√ Understand how to do quoting, paraphrasing, and summarizing,

√ Practice using correct in-text citations.

1 Critical Thinking Questions

Directions: Work in small groups and discuss the following open questions.

■ When you read one published research paper, why is it important to know where the authors have found its information?

■ Do you know what plagiarism is? How can you avoid plagiarism?

■ Do you know what is quoting and how to quote, what is paraphrasing and how to paraphrase, what is summarizing and how to summarize?

2 In-Text Citation VS. Plagiarism

Generally, plagiarism can be described as academic theft, which means scholars or students use others' ideas without giving them credit. This can happen accidentally (forgetting to indicate the source of the information), or it can happen deliberately.

Accidental plagiarism happens because you don't do proofreading or you are short of experience of the academic context. Deliberate plagiarism may be caused by a lack of confidence, which means the writer feels he or she is inferior to the author whose ideas and words are better than his or hers. However, even a few unacknowledged words in your text can be plagiarized, too.

Remember, there is no excuse for plagiarism, and that's why the word "theft" is used to describe it. If you plagiarize in your essay/research paper, it is always taken as an academic "crime". The punishment for plagiarism is quite severe, ranging from reducing an assignment grade to expulsion from university.

So how can we avoid plagiarism? The most useful method is in-text citation.

Activity 1 »

Directions: Plagiarism ranges from accidental plagiarism to deliberate plagiarism. Look at the following two passages. Evaluate the statements following each quoted passage and mark them S (satisfactory) or U (Unsatisfactory). Be prepared to explain what is wrong with those marked U.

Passage One

"Hoarding is a dark side to the human-animal bond that is vastly undiscovered," [Gary] Patronek says. "While most people may find hoarders' living conditions unbearable, the hoarders themselves see no problem, seeing their home as a safe-haven for the animals."

Source: Tremayne, Jessica. "Can You Identify Animal Hoarders? New Legislative Push Binds Practitioners to Report Cases", *DVM Newsmagazine* Feb. 2005: 12-13.

Statements:

_____ a. Most animal hoarders believe they are providing a "safe haven" for their animals, even though others see the situation as "unbearable". (Tremayne 12)

_____ b. Gary Patronek calls animal hoarding the "dark side to the human-animal bond". (Tremayne 12)

_____ c. Animal hoarders are often unable to recognize the terrible conditions in which they and their animals are living. (Tremayne 12)

Passage Two

Historically, what we today call the Underground Railroad was the process—by which slaves escaped northward to the free states, to Canada, or to points south, west and out to sea. Broadly, it consisted of the individual and collective actions of thousands of enslaved people who were trying to achieve liberty and a new beginning to their lives.

Source: Blight, David W. "The Underground Railroad in History and Memory", Introduction, *Passages to Freedom: The Underground Railroad in History and Memory*, Ed. David W. Blight. Washington: Smithsonian, 2004: 1-10.

Statements:

_____ a. David W. Blight broadly defined the Underground Railroad as the efforts made by slaves to escape to freedom and by those who helped them.

_____ b. Broadly speaking, the Underground Railroad was the process by which slaves attempted to escape to freedom.

_____ c. Although movies dealing with the Underground Railroad suggested that it was an elaborate, highly organized movement, David W. Blight emphasized that it often was not.

Activity 2 »

Directions: The following example shows accidental plagiarism. Can you find it?

For instance, some explicit regulations and rules like after-sales taxes repayment are commanded by supervisors and managers. Finally, contractual agreements are said to range from the "explicit" (formalized by printed contracts establishing legal bonds) to the "implicit" (the rules based on social behaviors). (Els, 2013, p. 106)

Answer

③ The Principles and Ways of In-Text Citation

A citation gives names of the author and work, and shows sufficient bibliographic information that the reader can track down the original source, so actually a citation is the act of identifying sources and shows attribution and respect to others' achievements. Sometimes students commit plagiarism just because they do not know how to cite others' ideas properly. Therefore, standard citation should meet the following principles:

Principles of standard citation:

Firstly, make sure to cite only the most appropriate, the latest and published literature.

Secondly, make sure to offer citations for direct quotations and ideas, paraphrases, and data taken from an original source.

Thirdly, make sure to guarantee accuracy in citation and standardization of the citation form.

Fourthly, try to be tentative in citation instead of being too assertive.

Fifthly, make sure to cite as you use and not to cite more than necessary.

Finally, avoid "catch-all" citation at the end of a paragraph.

Ways of in-text citation:

Whenever referring to another researcher' results, conclusion, or methods, you have to do citation. Generally speaking, the reference in the text is made only with the author's name and date of publication. There are three ways of doing this:

(1) Both the name and date are enclosed in parentheses. There is a comma between the author and year. Sometimes, the comma can be omitted according to different publishers' requirements.

For example:

A domain involves typical interactions between typical participants in typical settings (Holmes, 2011).

Because a domain involves typical interactions between typical participants in typical settings (Holmes, 2011), I think several domains can be identified in…

Additionally, one thing has to be pointed out, that is, the parentheses containing the reference are placed at the end of the sentence or clause and the punctuation follows the citation.

(2) Use the last name of the researcher as the subject or object of the sentence or clause and follow it immediately with the date of the study in parentheses.

For example:

Holmes (2011) defines a domain as typical interactions between typical participants in typical settings.

Because Holmes (2011) defines that a domain involves…

These data support the conclusions of Holmes (2011).

(3) Omit the parentheses, if you wish to emphasize the date of the cited study.

For example:

In the year of 2011 (or In 2011), Holmes defines a domain as typical interactions between typical participants in typical settings.

In addition, if there are more than one study you would like to cite per reference, i.e., more than one author has reached the same conclusion, you may list them together in the same parentheses and separate their names by semicolons. By convention, they are listed in chronological order. Moreover, in the case of more than three authors, you may use "et al." after the first author's name.

For example:

A domain has been defined as typical interactions between typical participants in typical settings (*Jones, 1989; Smith, 1999; Holmes, 2011*).

A domain is defined as typical interactions between typical participants in typical settings (*Jones et al, 1989*).

(Note: Please see Appendixes for more ways and principles.)

The Dancing Fox: A Sample Paper in APA Style（In-text Citations）

...

...

Paraphrasing is stating an idea of another's in one's own words. Quoting is stating another's exact words-both need to be cited. Include the author(s) and year for paraphrases and the author(s), year, and page or paragraph number for direct quotes. "When paraphrasing or referring to an idea contained in another work, you are encouraged to provide a page or paragraph number, especially when it would help an interested reader locate the relevant passage in a long or complex text" (APA, 2010, p. 171). Duvall, Walker, and Jensch (1996) explain that when quoting or paraphrasing authors outside of parenthetical citations, one refers to them by their last names and joins the last author with the second-to-last author with the word and spelled out. Words written as words should be italicized. Parenthetical citations and references join authors with an ampersand (&) rather than spelling out and (Duvall, Walker, & Jensch, 1996). Include the year in all parenthetical citations, even if it seems redundant (Duvall et al., 1996, para.1; APA, 2010, pp.174, 170, 174).

...

(Excerpted from *The Dancing Fox: A Sample Paper in APA Style by Minnie Ames*, 2013, p.3)

...

Activity 4 »

Directions: For in-text citation, there are in fact many style guidelines, including American Psychological Association (APA) Style, Modern Language Association (MLA) Style, and the Chicago Manual of Style (CMS) (More information seen in Appendix1, 2, 3). Please surf the Internet or read books to find the similarities and differences of these three styles.

Similarities	Differences

4 Quoting

There are two ways for you to use the materials from the sources: *indirect quotations* (summarizing and paraphrasing, presented without quotation marks) and *direct quotations* (quoting verbatim, or word for word, enclosed within quotation marks). No matter what mode of quotation you adopt, the sources must be indicated clearly, either with a superscript (raised number) in the text that refers to a note, as Chicago Manual Style proposes, or with a parenthetical reference in the text, as the MLA Style and APA Style prefer.

But this section only focuses on direct quotations, and in the following section, paraphrasing and summarizing (indirect quotations) will be discussed accordingly.

Definition of direct quotations

Direct quotation means presenting materials word for word from a source. When you wish to emphasize the accuracy of your material from the source, or summon the voice of an authority, direct quotation is appropriate and necessary.

Direct quotations should be kept as short as possible. If a very long quotation (more than one-half page of the text) is indispensable to your paper, you may place it in an appendix with a cross reference, otherwise it will overwhelm your discussion. Meanwhile you need to take into account the concept of *fair use* and secure the permission of the publisher or the copyright holder for some quotations.

Kinds of direct quotations

1) Short quotations:

According to Chicago Manual Style, if the quotation is fewer than one hundred words (approximately eight lines of text), it is enclosed in double quotation marks. MLA Style and APA Style use similar rule, but run in less quoted material: fewer than 40 words (roughly three or four lines of text). In a word, if the quotation is fewer than forty words, you should adopt it in the text directly and use double quotation marks (" "). What's more, you should indicate the page number after the quotation, if possible.

For example:

Noting that "plagiarism is not infrequently described as immoral" , Rebecca Howard Moore (1982) then quotes a number of prominent figures to illustrate her point (p.793).

2) Extended (Long) quotations:

In terms of Chicago Manual Style, an essay quotation of 100 words (roughly eight lines) or more should be taken from the text by indentation and double space, while MLA Style and APA Style indent and double-space essay quotations of 40 or more words.

> For example:
>
> Freshman English is a luxury that consumes time, money, and the intelligence of an army of young teachers and of younger teaching fellows. It imposes the standards of taste of a single discipline upon a freshman population whose command of language is sufficient to its purpose. It seldom solves the educational problems of the students with real inabilities to speak, to read, to write. . . . It would be better to stop what we are doing, to sit still, to rest in the sun, and then to search for the populations whose problems can be solved by our professional skills. (Irene L. Clark, 2008, p. 187)

However, for theses and dissertations, single-spacing is always preferred because it is more like a printed format. Mainly for APA style, if it is more than 40 words, put the quote in a freestanding block and indent the block approximately 1.3 cm from the left margin. Single-space the indented block (Dorothy et al., 2015).

> **NOTE:**
>
> When you use material from other sources, you must follow the guidelines of *fair use*. According to one rule of thumb, you may quote up to 150 words from a source, or two lines of poetry, for critical or evaluative purposes without obtaining permission from the copyright holder. In most cases, the copyright holder is the publisher (because the author has transferred the copyright to the publisher). Some publishers allow the quotation of 250 words without written permission; some allow up to 500 words.

扩展阅读: 7.1

Quoting

Activity 5 »

Directions: The following passage is quoted from Gibaldi (2001: 22). Read it first and then decide which example is plagiarizing and unacceptable, and which is acceptable. Then give reasons for your decision.

The following passage appears in Volume 1 of the *Literary History of the United States*.

The major concerns of Dickenson's poetry early and late, her "flood subject", may be defined as the season and nature, death and a problematic afterlife, the kinds and phases of love, and poetry as the divine art.

The followings are two examples:

1. The chief subjects of Emily Dickinson's poetry include nature and the seasons, death and the afterlife, the various types and stages of life, and poetry itself as a divine art.

2. Gilson and Williams suggest that the chief subjects of Emily Dickinson's poetry include nature, death, love, and poetry as a divine art (Zhencong Liu & Yuezhen Xiu, 2009, p.74).

Analysis

Activity 6 »

Directions: Write a short paragraph on the topic given. Use direct or indirect quotations for support, including some additional supporting sentences and transition signals to connect the ideas and make your paragraph flow smoothly.

Step 1: Copy the topic sentence exactly as it is given.

Step 2: Write several supporting sentences, using the main points and quotations supplied. Add supporting details such as examples if you can. Use the techniques and rules you have learned for direct and indirect quotations.

Step 3: Add an in-text citation in the proper format after each direct and indirect quotation.

Topic Sentence	The increased use of computers in business has been accompanied by a costly increase in computer crime.
Main Point A	Computer criminals cost business a lot of money.

Quotation	"The financial losses to business from computer thefts will exceed 25 billion dollars in 2005."
Main Point B	Computer criminals steal not only money but also information.
Quotation	"It is not just the money that they steal; they steal data, and data is power."
Source	A book written by Meredith Bruce, *Cybercrime*, page 185. The book was published in New York by a company named Wexler in 2004. (Source: Extract from *Writing Academic English*, 4th edition, by Alice Oshima and Ann Hogue, pp.49-50)

Completed Paragraph

5 Paraphrasing

For indirect quotations, there are also two methods: *paraphrasing* and *summarizing*. How to paraphrase in the writing without committing plagiarism? Apart from direct quotations, another effective way is *paraphrasing*.

Paraphrasing means you rewrite information from an outside source in your own words without changing the meaning. The following steps help you master the useful paraphrasing technique.

Techniques of paraphrasing:

Firstly, you have to decide how the ideas from the original text fit into your essay, and only use the relevant ideas.

Secondly, you have to read the original text again and again in order to understand its real meaning, and then put the original text away.

Thirdly, you have to write down the ideas about what the text says in your own words, and compare your wording and ideas with the original ones.

Lastly, you have to check whether your essay clarifies the text and builds on it.

In addition, there is one more point you have to notice. That is, paraphrasing doesn't mean substituting words for other words and changing the word order of the original sentence. If you do so, it results in too much of the original text being reproduced, which can commit plagiarism.

扩展阅读: 7.2

Paraphrasing

Activity 7 »

Directions: Look at the following two paraphrases and compare them with the original text. Do they express the same meaning and use the writers' own words? Which one is better? Why?

Original text

Pop culture and fashion have been influenced for many years by Eastern culture. In part, this is due to the flourishing textile industry in countries such as China, Pakistan and India.

Additionally, fashion has been inspired by colors and patterns that are prevalent in the East, with many Western designers including them in their ranges. [Taken from a book by Wood, published in 2011]

Paraphrase 1

China, Pakistan and India have had a great influence on the West. One example is their textile industry, which is growing and therefore influencing fashion and popular culture. Western designers are also using colors and patterns that influence the East (Wood, 2011).

Paraphrase 2

Clothing trends and popular culture have been affected for a long time by the culture from the East. The Chinese, Pakistani and Indian clothing industries are thriving, which can partly explain this influence. Moreover, stylists from the West have added Eastern colors and designs to their collections, which shows how the fashion industry has been influenced (Wood, 2011). (Source: Extracted from *Writing: Learn to Writing Better Academic Essays*, by Els Van Geyte, 2013.)

Answers

Activity 8 »

Directions: Read the original text carefully. After fully understanding it, paraphrase the original text. Then compare the original text with your paraphrase sentence by sentence, and at the same time, analyze how the sentence structure and words differ.

Original text

Language is the main means of communication between peoples. But as society developed, so many different languages have developed that language has therefore been a barrier rather than an aid to understanding among peoples. For many years, people have dreamed of setting up an international universal language which all people could speak and understand. The arguments in favor of a universal language are simple and obvious. If all peoples spoke the same tongue, cultural and economic ties might be much closer, and good will might increase between countries (Kispert).

(Source: Extract from *Writing Academic English*, 4th edition, by Alice Oshima and Ann Hogue, pp.137-138.)

Paraphrase

6 Summarizing

For indirect quotations, another way to use borrowed information from an outside source is to summarize it. The difference between paraphrase and summary is: When someone tells you a story, you retell it and repeat it in your own words. The length of your retelling is about the same as the original, and it is a paraphrase. While when you retell only the most important points and leave the details out by shortening the story, it is a summary. As to how to write a good summary, there are three keys to follow.

Keys of summarizing:

First, you have to use your own words and your own sentence structure.

Second, you have to remember that a summary, including only the main points and main supporting points, is much shorter than a paraphrase.

Third, you cannot change the meaning of the original.

Concrete steps for writing a summary:

First, read the original passage as many times as possible until you understand it completely.

Second, decide what the important ideas are and write notes with only several words, rather than complete sentences for each idea.

Third, write your summary from your notes, without looking at the original while you are writing.

Fourth, check your summary and make sure that your summary is against the original and you have not altered the original meaning, along with adding an in-text citation at the end of the summary.

扩展阅读: 7.3

Summarizing

Activity 9 »

Directions: Read the following original passage and the two summaries that follow it. Then answer the questions.

Original Passage

Swahili speakers wishing to use a "compyuta"—as *computer* is rendered in Swahili—have been out of luck when it comes to communicating in their tongue. Computers, no matter how bulky their hard drives or sophisticated their software packages, have not yet mastered Swahili or hundreds of other indigenous African languages.

But that may soon change. Across the continent, linguists are working with experts in information technology to make computers more accessible to Africans who happen not to know English, French, or the other major languages that have been programmed into the world's desktops.

There are economic reasons for the outreach. Microsoft, which is working to incorporate Swahili into Microsoft Windows, Microsoft Office, and other popular programs, sees a market for its software among the roughly 100 million Swahili speakers in East Africa. The same goes for Google, which last month launched www.googl.co.ke, offering a Kenyan version in Swahili of the popular search engine.

But the campaign to Africanize cyberspace is not all about the bottom line. There are hundreds of languages in Africa—some spoken only by a few dozen elders—and they are dying out at an alarming rate. The continent's linguists see the computers as one important way of saving them. UNESCO estimates that 90 percent of the world's 6,000 languages are not represented on the internet and that one language disappears somewhere around the world every two weeks.

(Source: Excerpted from a newspaper article written by Marc Lacey. It appeared on page A3 of the *New York Times* on November 12, 2004. The title of the article is "*Using a New Language in Africa to Save Dying Ones*".)

Summary A

People who speak Swahili want to communicate by using a "compyuta" , which is the Swahili word for computer, and are unable to do so in their own language. It makes no

---

difference that computers have huge hard drives and sophisticated software. They cannot operate in Swahili or other African languages, of which there are hundreds. Soon, however, they may be able to. Linguists in Africa are working with information technology specialists to make computers operable to Africans who do not know any of the languages currently used on the internet. Economics is bringing about this change. Microsoft sees a market for its software among Swahili speakers in East Africa. Google now has a search engine for speakers of Swahili in Kenya. Other software companies will probably soon develop products for African consumers. In addition to economics, there is another reason for making the computer accessible to Africans. Hundreds of African languages are dying out, and linguists view the computer as a way to save them. According to UNESCO estimates, 90 percent of the world's 6,000 languages are not on the Internet, and one language becomes extinct every day somewhere in the world. The hope is that computers can help save them (Lacey).

Summary B

Many Africans who do not speak any of the major languages on the Internet have been able to use computers in their native languages. Computers can not yet accommodate languages such as Swahili. However, that situation may soon change. Linguists and computer experts are working to develop computers that work in Swahili and other African languages. Economics is one reason for doing so. Computer companies such as Microsoft and Google see a potentially huge market for its products in Africa. Another important reason is to save languages that are in danger of becoming extinct (Lacey).

Questions:

1. Which of the two is the better summary? Why?

2. Which summary contains an idea that was not in the original? Which sentence expresses this added idea?

Activity 10 »

Directions: Write a one-paragraph summary of the following passage. The following steps are for you to resort to.

- Read the original passage several times until you understand it well. You may find it helpful to underline the main points.
- Make notes in the space provided, changing vocabulary words wherever possible.

- Write a summary of the passage in your own words.
- Add an in-text citation at the end of each summary.

Original Passage

"The world faces a future of people speaking more than one language, with English no longer seen as likely to become dominant", a British language expert says in a new analysis. "English is likely to remain one of the world's most important languages for the foreseeable future, but its future is more problematic and complex than most people appreciate," said language researcher David Graddol (Schmid, para. 1-2).

He sees English as likely to become the "first among equals" rather than having the global field to itself (para. 3).

The share of the world's population that speaks English as a native language is falling. Graddol reports in a paper in Friday's issue of the journal *Science* (para. 5).

"There is a distinct consciousness in many countries, both developed and developing, about this dominance of English; there is some evidence of resistance to it, a desire to change it", said [Scott] Montgomery (the author of another article published in the same issue of *Science*). For example, he said, "in the early years of the Internet it was dominated by sites in English, but in recent years there has been a proliferation of non-English sites, especially Spanish, German, French, Japanese, and others." (para. 19-20)

"Nonetheless, English is strong as a second language, and teaching it has become a growth industry." said Montgomery, a Seattle-based geologist and energy consultant (para. 21).

Graddol noted, though, that employers in parts of Asia were already looking beyond English, "In the next decade the new 'must learn' language is likely to be Mandarin " (para. 22).

(Source: Various paragraphs of a new article written by Randolph E. Schmid. It was published online by the Associated Press on February 26, 2004. The title of the article is "*Share of People who Are Native English Speakers Declining*" . The article is 25 paragraphs long.)

Put it Together

Directions: These are the important points covered in this chapter.

1. When writing an academic paper or essay, there are three styles for you to turn to, and they are:

_____

_____

_____

_____

_____

_____

2. In academic writing, you are expected to use information from outside source to support your ideas. In addition to using quotations, what other means can you refer to in order to avoid plagiarism?

_____

_____

_____

_____

_____

_____

3. Keep in your mind that the US system of education values student's original thinking and writing. Don't write a paper that contains only the ideas of others. So how do you use the outside sources to support your own ideas?

_____

_____

_____

_____

_____

_____

4. Don't just drop a paraphrase or summary into your paper. Make the connection between the borrowed information and your idea clear. How can you connect and make the idea clear?

_____

_____

_____

_____

_____

_____

_____

_____

Chapter 8
Writing the First Draft

In this chapter, you will know:

✓ How to write the first draft,

✓ How to write a thesis statement,

✓ How to write introduction, body and conclusion paragraphs.

1 Critical Thinking Questions

Directions: Work in small groups and discuss the following open questions.

■ How do you write the first draft? How many steps are there during the whole writing process?

How to write?

How many steps?

■ What are the major steps for college students to write academic essays?

■ What is the most essential step in academic writing? How do you carry it on?

■ Do you know the basic organization of a piece of academic writing? Please list it and explain specifically.

2 Thesis Statement

The most important sentence in the introduction is the thesis statement, which states the specific topic of the essay.

Generally, there are several rules for you to follow if you want to put forward a strong thesis statement, that is, a strong thesis takes some sort of stance. A strong thesis justifies discussion, expresses one main idea, and is relatively specific.

Thus, a well-expressed or strong thesis statement will guide or direct the reader, and provide him or her with a clear focus, by means of making the point specifically and effectively.

For example:

The large number of immigrant workers from rural to urban areas has major effects on cities.

Sometimes the subtopics are listed in a thesis statement that will be discussed in the body.

For example:

The large number of immigrant workers from rural to urban areas has major effects on a city's ability at providing housing, employment, and transportation.

Sometimes the pattern of organization is also shown in a thesis statement that the essay will follow. The following thesis statements show "logical division of ideas", "comparative and contrast" and "chronological order" patterns respectively.

For example:

If you are going to buy an old car, there are four strategies for you to follow, in order to get the best price.

There are many differences between Western table manners and Chinese table manners.

My uncle and aunt spend an entire summer travelling around the country by driving their van.

Activity 1 »

Directions: Study these thesis statements from two different essays on the topic of *The Status of Women in China*. One of the essays uses a comparison/contrast pattern, and the other a time sequence (chronological order) pattern. Which pattern do two statements indicate respectively?

1. From World War Ⅱ to contemporary China, the status of women in the society has changed dramatically.

Pattern of organization: _____

2. Although the status of women in China has improved dramatically in recent years, there is still a way to go, compared to the status of women in the western world.

Pattern of organization: _____

Activity 2 »

Directions: The following four thesis statements are all weak. Please work with your partner and talk about what rules you may follow and how to turn them into strong thesis statements.

> **Four kinds rules are as follows:**
>
> A strong thesis takes some sort of stance.
>
> A strong thesis justifies discussion.
>
> A strong thesis expresses one main idea.
>
> A strong thesis is relatively specific.

1. There are some negative and positive aspects to the Banana Herb Tea Supplement.

Strong thesis: _____

_____

_____

_____

2. My family is an extended family.

Strong thesis: _____

_____

_____

_____

3. Companies need to exploit the marketing potential of the Internet and Web pages can provide both advertising and customer support.

Strong thesis: _____

_____

_____

_____

4. World hunger has many causes and effects.

Strong thesis: _____

_____

_____

_____

When writing thesis statements, people often make mistakes that undermine their chances of producing an effective essay. One mistake is to simply announce the subject rather than state a true thesis. The second mistake is to write a thesis that is too broad, and the third is to write a thesis that is too narrow. The fourth mistake is to write a thesis containing more than one idea. Here are tips for avoiding such mistakes and writing good thesis statements.

Ways for avoiding mistakes in writing good thesis statements:

1) Write effective statements, not announcements.

Examples of announcements:

The subject of this paper will be my parents.

I want to talk about the crime wave in our country.

The baby-boom generation is the concern of this essay.

Examples of effective thesis statements:

My parents struggled with more energy for some reasons.

The recent crime wave in our city has several apparent causes.

The baby-boom generation has changed American society in key ways.

2) Avoid statements that are too broad.

Examples of too broad thesis statements:

Disease has shaped human history.

Insects are fascinating creatures.

Men and women are very different.

Revised thesis statements:

In the mid-1980s, AIDS changed people's attitudes about dating.

Strength, organization and communication make the ant one of the nature's most successful insects.

Men and women are often treated very differently in the workplace.

3) Avoid statements that are too narrow.

Examples of too narrow thesis statements:

The speed limit near my home is sixty-five miles per hour.

A hurricane hit southern Florida last summer.

A person must be at least thirty-five years old to be elected president of the United States.

Revised thesis statements:

The speed limit near my home should be lowered to fifty-five miles per hour for several reasons.

Federal officials made a number of mistakes in their response to the recent Florida hurricane.

The requirement that a U.S. president must be at least thirty-five years old is unfair and unreasonable.

4) Make sure the statements develop only with one idea.

Examples of the statements containing more than one idea:

One of the most serious problems affecting young people today is bullying and it is time more kids learned the value of helping others.

Studying with others has several benefits, but it also has drawbacks and can be difficult to schedule.

He has played an important role in my life, but he's not as important as her.

Revised thesis statements:

One of the most serious problems affecting young people today is bullying.

Studying with others has several benefits.

She (Teacher) has played an important role in my life.

Activity 3 »

Directions: Analyze the following thesis statements and rewrite them.

1. The way our society treats elderly people is unbelievable.

_____

_____

_____

2. Enrollment at Freestone State College increased by 10 percent.

_____

_____

_____

3. California has much to offer the tourist.

_____

_____

_____

4. I failed my biology course.

_____

_____

_____

3 Process to Write the First Draft

In the first draft writing, your important goal is to state your thesis clearly and develop your essay contents in logic, instead of taking the time to correct words or sentences that you may remove in your later writing. Thus, writing the first draft usually follows some necessary steps.

扩展阅读: 8.1

Writing the First Draft

Step 1 Prewriting

The first step in the writing process is to choose a topic and collect information about it. This step is often called prewriting because you do the step before you start writing. Here are two tips for you to do beforehand.

1) Choose a topic that interests you.

2) Choose a topic that fits the assignment.

For example: The diagram is showing how to narrow a topic of an essay.

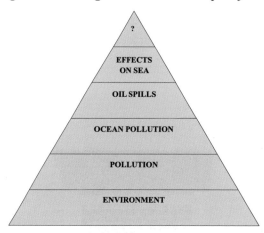

As is seen, the topic about ocean pollution is still too large because it includes pollution by oil, chemicals, sewage, and garbage. Therefore, you must narrow your topic further — perhaps to oil as a source of ocean pollution. You could also make this topic even narrower by writing only about the effects of oil spills on sea life. This is an appropriate topic for a college assignment, perhaps a ten-page paper. According to an essay length paper, you should narrow the topic further, perhaps to just one kind of sea life — corals or sea birds or shellfish. The diagram illustrates the process of narrowing a topic. For more information, please see Chapter 2.

Activity 4 »

Directions: Work individually to choose and narrow a topic by means of *Brainstorming* or *Clustering*, and then write freely on the following topics according to the prewriting step of first draft.

(1) School

(2) Entertainment

(3) Sports

(4) Food

Step 2　Outlining

After prewriting, the second step is outlining. Outlining is central for writing a good essay, which can be seen as the bare bones of an essay. As stated in Chapter 4, there are two types of outlining: key words outline and sentence outline. Outlining provides a quick check on whether your essay will be unified. It also suggests right at the start whether your essay will be adequately supported. And it shows you how to plan an essay that is well organized.

Activity 5 »

The following exercise will help you develop the outlining skills, which are very important to plan and write a solid essay. One key to effective outlining is the ability to distinguish between major ideas and supporting details that fit under those major ideas. In each of the following lists, major ideas and supporting items are mixed together.

Directions: Working in pairs, distinguish major ideas and supporting details. Please put the items into logical order of outlining.

1. Thesis: My high school had three problem areas.

Students/ Teachers

Unwilling to help after class

Formed cliques

Buildings

Ill-equipped gym

Much too strict

2. Thesis: Working as a dishwasher in a restaurant was the worst job to me.

Ten-hour shifts

Heat in kitchen

Working conditions

Minimum wage

Hours changed every week

No bonus for overtime

Hours

Pay

Noisy work area

Step 3　Drafting

Step 3 in the writing process is writing the rough draft. Follow your outline as closely as possible, and don't worry about grammar, punctuation, or spelling. A rough draft is not supposed to be perfect. Above all, remember that writing is a continuous process of discovery. As you are writing, you will think of new ideas that may not be in your brainstorming list or outline. You can add or delete ideas at any time in the writing process. Just be sure that any new ideas are relevant and guided by the unity of the thesis. A rough draft that a student writes should be in accordance with the outline and single thesis statement.

Step 4   Polishing

After you write the rough draft, another step is to revise it. When you revise, you change and improve what you have written. You check it for content and organization, including unity, coherence, and logic. You can change, rearrange, add, or delete, for the goal of communicating your thoughts in a clearer, more effective and more interesting way.

During the first revision, do not try to correct grammar, sentence structure, spelling, or punctuation, which is proofreading, and you will do it later. During the first revision, be concerned mainly with content and organization.

Read over your paragraph carefully for a general overview. Focus on the general aspects of the paper and make notes in the margins about rewriting parts that need to be improved.

- Check to see that you have achieved your stated purpose.
- Check for general logic and coherence. Your audience should be able to follow your ideas easily and understand what you have written.
- Check to make sure that your paragraph has a topic sentence and that the topic sentence has a central (main) focus.
- Check to make sure that the topic sentence is developed with sufficient supporting details. Does each paragraph give the reader enough information to understand the main idea? If the main point lacks sufficient information, make notes in the margin such as "add more details" or "add an example".
- Check for unity. Cross out sentences that are off the topic.
- Check your use of transition signals.
- Finally, check your paragraph to make sure that it has or needs a concluding sentence. If you write a final comment, is it on the topic?

Activity 6 »

Directions: Write your first draft based on the outline you have prepared before, and then revise the draft with the help of the previous checklist.

4 Practice for the Introductory Paragraphs

Functions of Introductory Paragraph

　　1. It attracts the readers, interest, encouraging them to continue reading the essay.

　　2. It supplies any background information that readers may need to understand the essay.

　　3. It presents a thesis statement. This clear and direct statement of the main idea of the paper usually appears near the end of the introductory paragraph.

　　4. It indicates a plan of essay development. Here, the major supporting points for the thesis. In some cases, the thesis and plan of development appear in the same sentence.

Activity 7 »

Directions: Work individually and finish questions according to 3 steps, and then share your draft with a partner.

　　Step 1: Read each of the following sets of sentences. Put them in the correct order to form introductory paragraphs.

　　Step 2: Write each paragraph, beginning with the most general statement first, and then arrange each sentence in the correct order until the introduction becomes more specific with appropriate connecting words and signal words. Write the thesis statement last.

　　Step 3: Identify the type of introduction ("funnel", dramatic/interesting/funny story, surprising statistics, or historical event, and so on).

　　Paragraph 1

　　1. If being done properly, a handshake gives the impression of strength and honesty, and if being done improperly, it conveys weakness and dishonesty.

　　2. In some cultures, people bow, and in others, they shake hands.

　　3. In English-speaking countries, shaking hands is the custom.

4. A proper handshake has four ingredients: pressure, pumps, eye contact, and verbal message.

5. The way people greet each other when they meet for the first time varies from culture to culture.

6. How one shakes hands sends an important message about one's character.

Type of introduction: _____

Paragraph 2

1. To celebrate the occasion, Mr. X decided to hold a big party at the plant.

2. Mr. X went to Mexico from England to manage a milk plasticization plant.

3. Then one day an impressive new pasteurization unit arrived and was installed.

4. The employees did most of the planning and draped the new unit with garlands.

5. During the party, one of Mr. X's supervisors took him aside and said, "Now we see that you are a good and trusty person; from now on I am sure everyone will really try to do their best for you."

6. And so it was — neither punctuality nor quality checks were any longer needed.

7. This story illustrates the need to understand that doing business in a different culture demands an understanding of the culture.

8. The party was a great success, and everybody had a good time.

9. For eight months, he tried every way possible to convince his workers of the importance of punctuality and of checking every detail of their work.

10. The response was always, "Yes, yes, we will do our best", but nothing ever changed.

Type of introduction: _____

Paragraph 3

Note: The order of sentences 2, 3, and 4 can be rewritten.

1. Currently there are four main methods for predicting when and where the next Big One will occur.

2. In 1976, an earthquake in Tangshan, China, killed over 250000 people.

3. In an average year, earthquakes kill 10000 people worldwide and cause millions of dollars

worth of property damage.

4. Iran suffered more than 80,000 deaths in two massive quakes in 1996 and 2003.

5. Scientists keep trying to find ways to predict earthquakes — so far without success.

Type of introduction: _____

5 Practice for Body Paragraphs

Functions of Body Paragraphs

The body paragraphs in an essay are like the supporting sentences in a paragraph, which can develop your topic and prove your points. You should organize body paragraphs according to some patterns, such as chronological order or comparison/contrast. Sometimes, depending on your topic, you will need to use a combination of those patterns.

A basic pattern for essays is the logical division of ideas. In this pattern, you divide your topic into subtopics and then discuss each subtopic in a separate paragraph. Logical division is an appropriate pattern for explaining causes, reasons, types, qualities, methods, advantages and disadvantages, just as the typical college exam questions ask you to do.

Here are four keys to organize a logical division essay:

1. Divide your topic into subtopics, and then discuss each subtopic in a separate paragraph.

2. Write a thesis statement that indicates logical division.

3. Use transitions between paragraphs to guide your readers from one subtopic to the next.

4. Make the essay be coherent with types of logical and developmental methods.

Activity 8 »

Directions: Work in pairs and read the following paragraphs. And then write a coherent essay with transitions between body paragraphs. After that, write an outline for this essay.

Icebergs: A Potential Source of Water

1. In countries where rainfall is very small in amount, scientists must constantly seek ways to increase supplies of water. One method being considered is the use of desalination plants, which would remove salt from seawater. Another method being considered is the towing of icebergs. According to this method, large icebergs from Antarctica would be wrapped in cloth or plastic, tied to powerful tugboats by strong ropes, and towed to the countries needing freshwater. While this plan may have some potentials, there are certain practical problems that must be solved.

2. The first problem is the expense. According to estimates, it would cost between $50 million and $100 million to tow a single 100-million-ton iceberg from Antarctica to, for example, the coast of Saudi Arabia.

3. _____ is the possibility that the iceberg would melt during the journey. No one knows if an iceberg could be effectively insulated for such a long journey. At the very least, there is the possibility that it would break up into smaller pieces, which would create still other problems.

4. _____ there is the danger that a huge block of ice floating off an arid coast could have unexpected environmental effects. The ice could drastically change the weather along the coast, and it would probably affect the fish population.

5. _____ the cost of providing freshwater from icebergs would be less than the cost of providing water by desalinization, according to most estimates. It would cost between 50 and 60 cents per cubic meter to get water from an iceberg, as opposed to the 80 cents per cubic meter it would cost to get the same amount by desalinization.

6. In conclusion, before icebergs can become a source of freshwater in the future, problems involving cost, overall practicality, and most importantly, environmental impact must be solved.

6 Practice for the Concluding Paragraphs

Functions of Concluding Paragraph

1. It signals the end of the essay. To do so, begin your conclusion with a transition signal.

2. It reminds your readers of your main points, which you can do in one of two ways: summarizing your subtopics or paraphrasing your thesis.

3. It leaves your readers with your final thoughts on the topic. This is your opportunity to convey a strong, effective message that your readers will remember.

Some techniques used to write a memorable conclusion:

1. Make a prediction.

2. Suggest results or consequences.

3. Suggest a solution, make a recommendation, or call for action.

4. Quote an authority on the topic.

5. List the limitations of the work.

 **Activity 9** »

Step 1: Read the following two concluding paragraphs and answer the questions.

Concluding Paragraph A

To sum up, for culture shock, it is a very real phenomenon that has been studying for more than 30 years by anthropologists, psychologists and culture scholars, etc. There are possibly five phases which are positive feelings toward the new culture: awareness of small differences, growing discomfort and need for contact with home culture, negative feelings, acceptance and adjustment. Meanwhile, symptoms may vary, and not all people will need to experience all five phases. In the end, however, people who have suffered from culture shock are easily going to become stronger for having overcome the difficulties and frustrations of adapting to a new life in a new land.

Concluding Paragraph B

In conclusion, nearly everyone moving to a new country feels culture shock to a certain extent. Symptoms may vary, and not absolutely all people in a new land will experience all of the five stages. Newcomers supported by a strong group may feel at ease immediately in the new culture; while others may take weeks and months or longer to feel at home. To stay in touch with friends and family domestically, to keep a positive and optimistic attitude, and, above all, to learn the target language as quickly as possible are most effective ways to overcome the difficulties and frustrations of adapting to a new life in a new land.

Questions:

1. Which concluding paragraph is a summary of the supporting points? Give your reasons.
2. Which one is aiming at paraphrasing the thesis statement? Explain your point.

Step 2: Further Thinking

Think about the possible features in concluding paragraphs and complete the table by ticking (√) the appropriate columns.

Summary table:

Features in Concluding Paragraph(s)	Feature Contents	Ticking Feature(s)
Feature 1	Summarizing the supporting points	
Feature 2	Repeating the general statement	
Feature 3	Commenting on these ideas	
Feature 4	Making predictions for future developments of the topic	
Feature 5	Evaluating by giving suggestions of further research	
Feature 6	Listing the limitations of the work in the paragraphs	
Feature 7	Quoting an authority on the topic.	

Self-Evaluation

You are going to have a further evaluation in this part on the basis of what you have learned in this chapter. Therefore, please at first think back the major contents you have got and then finish the following evaluation exercise parts.

- **Directions: Please develop Body Paragraphs and finish Concluding Paragraph.**

Controlling Stress

Introductory Paragraph

The busy schedules that most adults face every day have created a growing health problem in the modern world. Stress affects almost everyone, from the highly pressured executives to the busy homemakers or students. It can cause a variety of physical disorders ranging from headaches to stomach ulcers and even alcoholism. Stress, like the common cold, is a problem that cannot be cured; however, it can be controlled. A person can learn to control stress in four ways.

Topic Sentences for Body Paragraphs

A. Set realistic goals.

B. Take up a hobby.

C. Exercise regularly.

D. Maintain close relationships with family and friends.

Concluding Paragraph _____

• **Directions: Write a first draft entitled "*On the Importance of Team Spirit and Communication in the Workplace*" on the basis of what you have learned in this chapter, and then do a peer-review work in pairs.**

(1) An introduction to the background information.

(*Please focus on delivering the thesis statement in this part.*)

(2) Making comments on the importance of team spirit.

(*Please use contrast in this part.*)

(3) Making comments on the importance of communication in the workplace.

(*Please use listing in this part.*)

(4) A conclusion part.

(*Please focus on how to make an ending in this part.*)

Chapter 9

Abstract and References

In this chapter, you will know:

√ How to write abstract,

√ Format of references,

√ What APA is,

√ APA formatting guide.

1 Critical Thinking Questions

Directions: Work in small groups and discuss the following questions.

■ Do you know what an abstract is? And its function in academic writing?

■ In an academic essay, how do you write a summary? Share your ideas.

■ Have you heard about APA or MLA? What are they?

2   How to Write an Abstract?

An abstract is a summary of a scientific essay or a research paper. It covers the main points of a piece of writing. Usually, an abstract should be concise, objective and complete. To write a good abstract, some elements of an abstract will be given as follows.

扩展阅读: 9.1

Abstract

- What does an abstract contain?

    1. Background information/Literature review;

    2. Principal purposes:

        What is the problem to be solved?

        What has been done?

        What are the results?

    3. Methodology;

    4. Research findings;

    5. Conclusions, recommendation, implication.

- To write a good abstract, the following questions are required to mention.

    1. What do you want to do in this essay?

    2. How did you do it?

    3. What results did you get and what conclusions could you draw?

    4. What is new and original in this essay?

Additionally, the abstract should never give any information or conclusion that is not stated in the academic essay. The language should be familiar to the potential readers, omitting obscure abbreviations. Draft and edit the essay before you write the abstract.

Here are the examples of abstracts, to help you have a thorough understanding of abstract format and demonstrate how to write an abstract.

Sample:

background

Feedback and assessment play an important role in teaching and learning of oral presentation skills. This study describes the implementation and evaluation of an innovative instruction that uses a Student Response System for peer assessment of oral presentations. A large number of oral presentations were assessed and students' perceptions and learning progress concerning the particular instructional approach were investigated. Results showed that the Student Response System was an effective way to produce feedback for presenters, assessors and educators. Results also revealed a very positive students' attitude towards the instructional format. The learning effect concerning assessment was rather limited. Further research is needed to come to conclusive statements about the latter.

what

method

results

recommendation

thesis

background

Third-hand Smoke

The harm of smoking has long been studied by researchers and many people are aware that second-hand smoke is harmful to nonsmokers, especially children. This study seeks to identify tobacco toxins that are invisible and its focus is on the risks those chemicals pose to infants and children. In this research, the term "third-hand smoke" was first used to describe the invisible yet poisonous gasses and particles that remain in houses or cars, including heavy metal and radioactive materials. And a survey was conducted on attitudes towards smoking in 1,500 households across the United States. It found that the vast majority of both smokers and nonsmokers were aware of the harm of second-hand smoke to children but a comparatively smaller part of them recognized the risks of third-hand smoke.

process

method

results

To write a good abstract of one academic essay, some rules should be known.

■ **Rules to follow:**

- Be of 100-300 words.
- Don't include details like examples.
- Don't quote or cite.
- Use present tense, past tense and present perfect tense.
- Specify any abbreviations.
- Use objective, academic instead of emotional words and expressions.

Activity 1 »

Directions: Work in pairs and distinguish the elements of the abstract below.

An Assessment of Consumer Attitudes Toward Direct Marketing Channels: A Comparison Between Unsolicited E-mail and Direct Mail

Abstract: The paper examines consumer attitudes towards two major direct marketing methods, unsolicited e-mail and postal direct mail. Psychological Reactance Theory was used to determine what factors might influence consumers' attitudes toward each communication method. Focus groups were conducted to discover the common themes and to identify the influential factors. The results of this study indicated that in comparison, unsolicited e-mail was more problematic than postal direct mail due to the inconvenience that spam presented to consumers.

Keywords: direct marketing, unsolicited e-mail spam, focus groups

Activity 2 »

Directions: Work individually, and write a draft of your abstract according to the rules and elements of an abstract.

3 Introduction of Reference

In academics and scholarship, a reference or bibliographical reference is a piece of information provided in a footnote or bibliography of a written work such as a book, article, essay, report, oration or any other text type, specifying the written work of another person used in the creation of that text. A bibliographical reference mostly includes the full name of the author, the title of their work and the year of publication.

A reference list lists only the sources you refer to in your academic writing. *The primary purpose of the reference list* is to allow your sources to be found by your reader. It also gives credit to the authors you have consulted for their ideas. All references cited in the text must appear in the reference list, except for personal communications (such as conversations or emails) which cannot be retrieved.

Source Type Options:

Do you know what you're citing? Answering this question is usually the first step in creating a reference. Usually, you can choose to cite from a list of 30+ source types, such as a website, book, video, online image, or something. How do you cite for different sources?

Do you know elements of reference formatting for different source types? Some common reference sources guides are as follows.

1. Journals

Author, Title of the article, Abbreviated Journal Name, Year, Volume, Page Range, DOI or other identifier. Available online: accessed on Day, Month, Year.

2. Books

Author, Book Title, Publisher, Publisher Location, Country, Year, Page Range.

3. Chapters

Author, Title of the chapter, Book Title, Editor, Publisher, Publisher Location, Country, Year, Volume, Page Range.

4. Unpublished Work

Author, Title of Unpublished Work, Abbreviated Journal Name, Stage of Publication (accepted; in press).

5. Personal Communication

Author, University/Institution/Organization, City, State/Province, Code, Telephone Number, Email Address.

6. Thesis or Dissertation

Author, Title of Thesis, Level of Thesis,

Degree-Granting University, Location of University,

Date of Completion.

7. Proceedings

Author, Proceedings of the Name of the Conference, Location of Conference, Country, Date of Conference.

Many professional organizations and publications have developed their own rules for formatting documents and citing sources. As a result, writers in different disciplines may decide which documentation style is suitable and right for you. Possibly, you've been given a specific citation style to use by your teacher, publication, editor, or colleague. If not, try APA citation, MLA format, Chicago referencing, or CSE citation as they are the most popular and commonly used in the various academic disciplines.

- **APA** style: This style, from the American Psychological Association, is used mainly in the social sciences — psychology, sociology, anthropology, political science, economics, education, and so on. (For more information, See Appendix 1.)

- **MLA** style: This style, from the Modern Language Association, is used primarily in the humanities — arts, English, philosophy, linguistics, world languages, and so on. (For more information, See Appendix 2.)

- **Chicago** style: Developed by the University of Chicago Press, this style is used primarily in history, journalism, and the humanities. (For more information, See Appendix 3.)

In all, your choice of documentation system will be guided by the discipline or field within which you are writing and by any requirements associated with your research writing project. For more information of reference formatting guides, please see Appendixes 1, 2 and 3.

Activity 3 »

Directions: Work in a small group and discuss these open-answered questions.

(1) What professional articles, papers and thesis have you ever read? Please name several of them.

_____

_____

_____

(2) If you cite a quotation from a published paper in your academic writing, what are you required to do?

_____

_____

_____

(3) How do you prepare the reference list?

_____

_____

_____

(4) Can you tell some differences between APA, MLA and Chicago style?

_____

_____

_____

4 APA Reference Format

There are several documentation systems, but the one currently most accepted for the social sciences and some of the natural sciences is the *APA style*. Developed by *the American Psychological Association*, *APA style* emphasizes the author(s) and publication date of a source. Writers use the APA documentation system to cite or formally acknowledge the information within their text by using parentheses, which is called in-text citation; and to provide a list of sources at the end of their document is called a reference list. Therefore, APA style requires that sources are cited in two ways: in-text citation and reference (or documentation). For more information about APA style, consult Appendix 1 or *the Publication Manual of the American Psychological Association* (*Sixth Edition*).

For the general requirements of *APA reference formatting guide*, see the following table. For more reference examples, please see Appendixes 1, 2 and 3.

APA Reference Formatting Guide	
Title	Include the title of "Reference" (beginning with a capital letter).
Indent	Hanging indent for your references (space bar in 5-7 spaces for the second and subsequent lines of each reference).
Space between references	In general, double-space between references.
Ampersand	For 2-6 authors, use "&" before the final author.
One author, two publications	Order by year of publication, and the earlier one first. Same year of publication for both — add "a" and "b" after the year, inside the brackets. Include this in text citation. Example: Baheti, J. R. (2001a).
URLs	Remove the underlines from URLs so that any underscores (_) can be seen.
Same first author, different second author	Order alphabetically by second or subsequent authors.
Upper case letters (capital letters)	Journal title—use headline style; i.e. capitalize all the words, except articles and prepositions; Book title or article title (in a journal, magazine or newspaper)—use sentence style; i.e. capitalize the first word of the title, subtitle (after the colon), and any proper names.
Place of publication	USA publishers give the city in full and the abbreviation for the state. For example: New York, NY / Springfield, MA. Publishers outside the USA: Give the city in full and the country in full. For example: London, England / Auckland, New Zealand.
Page range	Use an en dash, NOT a hyphen, for page ranges, e.g. 21–27. No gaps between the page numbers and the en dash. How to add an en dash in Microsoft Word? If using a full PC keyboard, hold the *Control* key and type the *minus sign* on the small numeric keypad.

APA Reference Formatting Guide	
Use of square brackets	If format, medium or description information is important for a resource to be retrieved or identified, use square brackets after the title to include this detail, for example: Scorsese, M. (Producer), & Lonergan, K. (Writer/Director). (2000). *You can count on me* [Motion picture]. United States: Paramount Pictures.

The Dancing Fox: A Sample Paper in APA Style

（In-text Citations and References）

...

...

Paraphrasing is stating an idea of another's in one's own words. Quoting is stating another's exact words — both need to be cited. Include the author(s) and year for paraphrases and the author(s), year, and page or paragraph number for direct quotes. "When paraphrasing or referring to an idea contained in another work, you are encouraged to provide a page or paragraph number, especially when it would help an interested reader locate the relevant passage in a long or complex text" (APA, 2010, p. 171). Duvall, Walker, and Jensch (1996) explain that when quoting or paraphrasing authors outside of parenthetical citations, one refers to them by their last names and joins the last author with the second-to-last author with the word and spelled out. Words written as words should be italicized. Parenthetical citations and references join authors with an ampersand (&) rather than spelling out *and* (Duvall, Walker, & Jensch, 1996). Include the year in all parenthetical citations, even if it seems redundant (Duvall et al., 1996, para.1; APA, 2010, pp.174, 170, 174).

...

...

Handouts, lecture notes, and PowerPoint presentations are treated like personal communications unless they are published in material that can be retrieved, like on a website or in a hard copy that is available to all readers (Zilcher, 2006). When citing a PowerPoint presentation, list the author, the copyright year (or n.d. if there is no date), and the slide number if it is a direct quote. "Vixens can leap higher than male fox"(Stinchfield, 2006, Slide 2). Koobel's Model of Experiential Learning (M. Teacher, personal communication, September

6, 2007) is a handout from class, so it is treated as a personal communication. "Foxes tire of dancing," according to a Bulletin Board message posted by Zoel Ming (2005). List a television show's script writer and director as the author(s) and the producer as editor.

...

...

(Excerpted from *The Dancing Fox: A Sample Paper in APA Style by Minnie Ames*, 2013, pp.3, 5.)

References

1. American Psychological Association. (2010). *Publication Manual of the American Psychological Association* (6th ed.). Washington, DC: American Psychological Association.

2. American Psychological Association. (2010). *Publication Manual of the American Psychological Association* (6th ed.). Washington, DC: American Psychological Association.

3. Duvall, L., Walker, J. S., & Jensch, C. (1996). *Fox Grammar*. Boston, MA: Apricot Binding.

4. Ming, Z. (2005, June 21). Foxes? [Online forum comment 182]. Retrieved from http://concordia.csp.edu/COBOL/MKM.marketing_strategies.

5. Stingchfield, E. L. (2006, April). "Dance" of the fox [lecture]. Retrieved from Dance World website: http://dance_Fox.ppt.

6. Zilcher, W. (2006). Lecture 10: Importance of Protecting the Fox[PowerPoint slides]. Retrieved from Cooper University Animal School website: http://cuas.courses.fox/lecture.cfm.

Activity 4 ≫

Directions: Work in pairs and define what the APA style refers to and summarize the features of the APA style which should be paid attention to in academic writing.

Activity 5 »

Directions: Work with a partner and label each part of the following references, using the key words that appear in most sources.

Key Words in Most Sources		
1. authors	2. editors	3. translators
4. book title	5. magazine title	6. article/chapter title
7. journal name	8. year of publication	9. date of publication
10. date of retrieval	11. volume /issue number	12. publisher
13. page numbers	14. city of publication	15. Database/Web name

1. Sheril, R. D. (1956). *The terrifying future: Contemplating color television.* San Diego: Halstead.

2. Smith, J., & Peter, Q. (1992). *Hairball*: *An intensive peek behind the surface of an enigma.* Hamilton, ON: McMaster University Press.

3. Mcdonalds, A. (1993). Practical methods for the apprehension and sustained containment of supernatural entities. In G. L. Yeager (Ed.), *Paranormal and occult studies*: *Case studies in application* (pp. 42–64). London: OtherWorld Books.

4. Crackton, P. (1987). *The Loonie*: *God's long-awaited gift to colourful pocket change*? Canadian Change, 64(7), 34–37.

5. Revenue Canada. (2001). *Advanced gouging*: *Manual for employees* (pp. 65–347/1124). Ottawa: Minister of Immigration and Revenue.

6. Marlowe, P., Spade, S., & Chan, C. (2001). *Detective work and the benefits of colour versus black and white* [*Electronic version*]. Journal of Pointless Research, 11,123–124.

7. Rogers, B. (2018). *Faster-than-light travel: What we've learned in the first twenty years.* Retrieved August 24, 2019, from Mars University, Institute for Martian Studies 14.

8. Hedges, C. (2009, May 4). Buying brand Obama. Truthdig. Retrieved October 2, 2009. From http: //www. truthdig.com/report/item/20090503buying_brand_ .

9. Fairclough, N. L. (1998). Political discourse in the media: An analytical framework. In A. Bell & P. Garrett (Eds.) *Approaches to Media Discourse* (pp. 142-161). Oxford: Blackwell Publishers Ltd.

5 Self-Evaluation

For each statement below, circle the word which is true for you.

1. I understand what abstract is.	Agree	Disagree	Not sure
2. I understand what summary is.	Agree	Disagree	Not sure
3. I know the differences between abstract and summary.	Agree	Disagree	Not sure
4. I understand what reference is.	Agree	Disagree	Not sure
5. I know reference is an unnecessary part of essay.	Agree	Disagree	Not sure
6. I can find key words in abstract and understand what I am expected to write.	Agree	Disagree	Not sure
7. I know what APA format refers to.	Agree	Disagree	Not sure
8. I know the differences between citation and reference.	Agree	Disagree	Not sure
9. I know how to take use of APA format in academic writing.	Agree	Disagree	Not sure
10. I know how to take use of MLA format in academic writing.	Agree	Disagree	Not sure

Chapter 10

Revising and Editing the Final Draft

In this chapter, you will know:

√ How to revise and edit your final draft,

√ The procedures of revising and editing your draft,

√ The focus of revising and editing the final draft,

√ How to proofread your draft.

1 Critical Thinking Questions

Directions: Work in small groups and discuss the following open questions.

- How many times do you think a thesis should be revised? Give your reasons.

- Should a thesis be revised starting from the macro aspects like structure and organization or from micro aspects such as grammar and spelling? Why?

- What are the resources or technologies that are helpful to revise your rough draft?

- What strategies should you use to revise and edit your final draft?

② General Introduction to Revising and Editing

When writers revise and edit, they evaluate the effectiveness of their first draft and, if necessary, work to improve them. Although the two processes are related, they focus on different aspects of an academic writing draft. **Revising** involves assessing how well a document responds to a specific writing situation, presents a main point and reasons to accept that point, and uses evidence. **Editing** includes evaluating and improving the expression—at the sentence and word levels—of the information, ideas, and arguments in the draft.

拓展阅读：10.1

Why or why won't you revise your manuscript?

Different focuses of revising and editing the draft document:

Focus of revising:

- The writing situation
- The argument and ideas
- The use and integration of sources
- The structure and organization
- The genre and design

Focus of editing:

- Accuracy
- Economy
- Consistency
- Style
- Spelling, grammar, and punctuation

Different strategies used for revising and editing the draft document:

Strategies used for revising:

- Save multiple drafts.
- Highlight your main point, reasons, and evidence.
- Challenge your assumptions.
- Scan, outline, and map your draft.
- Ask for feedback.

Strategies used for editing:

- Read carefully.
- Mark and search your draft for accuracy, consistency and language errors.
- Use spelling, grammar and style tools with caution.
- Ask for feedback.
- Consider genre and design.

For how to revise the rough draft, more information will be explained from *Chapter 3 to 8*.

③ Rereading Your Rough Draft

As writers revise, they should carve out from generalities to details, so there are several steps for revising and editing the final draft.

The first step to revise your final draft is rereading your rough draft globally for several times. "There is no great writing, only great re-writing," said Louis Brandeis. But, are the more revisions the better? Usually a thesis might be submitted after revision for three times at least.

How to reread your rough draft?

First, before starting to reread your rough draft, print it out and put it away. Give yourself a short break from the task by going out for a walk or listening to some light music. This break is essential to reset your mind by putting yourself in the shoes of your reader. Putting the writing in a different format by printing it out than revising it in a computer will help you critique your own work and give you a reader's perspective.

Second, reading your thesis out loudly is also a good way to check the fluency and meaning of each section in your rough draft. Listening to your written syntax is one of the best ways you can catch areas with awkward phrasing.

Third, make a mental note of any sentences or sections that do not make sense or that you stumble over while reading.

As a whole, rereading globally means looking at the big picture to address issues like thesis, evidence, audience, context, genre, organization and ethical responsibilities. After rereading, you may find some focuses possibly to revise for next step.

Activity 1 »

Directions: Print out your rough draft and read it out loudly, and then highlight those areas which sound awkward.

4   Revising the Overall Structure

Revising and editing the final draft usually starts from macro aspects to micro ones. The second step of editing the final draft is to revise the overall structure. Start your revision from taking a whole view of your rough draft by thinking over the following questions:

- **Is the title appropriate for the content?**

When revising your rough draft, a better title may jump into your mind since you have completed the writing and are fully clear about what you want to present in your paper.

- **Is the title interesting and attractive?**

Never bore the audience by using a cliché title.

- **Does your paper have a strong and clear central idea which is well supported and developed?**

When revising, you should assess whether the central idea is supported by the main ideas. Are main ideas supported by credible facts and examples?

- **Is the structure well organized?**

While revising the draft, you should think over whether all chapters and sections are closely related to the central idea and arranged logically. Is the sequence of the chapters needed to be reconstructed?

- **Are all essential parts available in your paper?**

Namely, title page, acknowledgement, abstract, table of contents, introduction, body part, conclusion, references and appendixes may be included in the final draft.

- **Is the format formal enough?**

Do you follow the format requirements including layout and font size? Do you obey the rules of MLA or APA to make sure the citations are not only correctly appeared in the body parts but also listed in order correspondingly in the references page of your paper?

Activity 2 »

Directions: Work in a small group and discuss the following open-answered critical thinking questions.

(1) How do you make your title interesting and attractive?

(2) Do you know how to focus on your responsibilities to the audience and yourself?

5 Revising Sections/Chapters

Warm-up: Tense and Voice in Thesis

Directions: It is an essential step to make sure that the tense and voice are in consistency and appropriately used in the thesis when revising the thesis section by section or chapter by chapter. Work in small groups and match each part of the thesis with correct tense.

a. Abstract

b. Introduction   Present tense

c. Literature review

d. Methodology

e. Results

f. Discussion   Past tense

g. Conclusion

The main body of the paper consists of several sections and chapters which indicate the development of central ideas. When revising, make sure that all chapters/sections support the thesis and that all details in each chapter/section support the chapter's/section's main idea. So how do we revise sections/chapters?

How to revise sections/chapters:

First, the sequence of sections or chapters may be rearranged in revision to ensure the progression of the central ideas in right direction.

Second, transitions between paragraphs in a chapter are also essential to ensure the smooth and logical flow of ideas.

Third, special attention should also be paid to the application of formal language such as the correct use of tone, tense, voice, third-person point of view and authoritative expressions which can make your paper look like objective and neutral.

To revise sections/chapters, carefully consider the following questions:

1) Are there any paragraphs in this section/chapter misplaced?

2) Are there any sections or ideas that need to be cut off or added in this chapter?

3) Is there a main topic in this section/chapter? Do all paragraphs support the main topic of this section/chapter?

4) Is every possible aspect of the topic or subject presented in this section /chapter?

5) Are the transitions between paragraphs logical and natural?

6) Is the tense and voice appropriate? Are they in consistency throughout the writing? In general, verb tense should be in the following format, although variations can occur within the text depending on the writing style of your paper. Note that references to prior research mentioned anywhere in your paper should always be stated in the past tense.

- Abstract—past tense [the summary description of what you did];
- Introduction—present tense [you are describing the study to reader now];
- Literature review—past tense [the studies you reviewed had already been written];
- Methodologies—past tense [the way you gathered and synthesized data had already happened];
- Results—past tense [the findings have already been discovered];
- Discussions—present tense [you are talking to reader now about how you interpret the findings];
- Conclusion—present tense [you are summarizing the study now].

7) Do you use the third-person point of view to make your thesis more objective? Generally speaking, the third-person point of view is considered to be more objective and formal than the first-person point of view in research papers.

8) Do you make your thesis authoritative? Are there any uncertain expressions, like "it seems to be..." or "it is said that...", in your draft which may give the impression to readers that your paper is not reliable?

Activity 3 »

Directions: Work in a small group and discuss the following open-ended questions.

(1) Is there any way to make your paper more objective? If any, what are they?

(2) How do you make your thesis authoritative?

6 Revising Paragraphs

Your writing is a reflection of your ideas and attitude toward your topic and audience. Thus, make sure that your paragraphs and sentences reflect the central idea and are appropriate for your writing situation.

How to revise paragraphs:

First, to revise a paragraph, you should make sure that each paragraph has a main point, and all sentences in this paragraph are subordinate to this main idea. If you can't figure out why you include a certain paragraph in your writing, this is a sign that it needs to be changed or left out. When a topic is well developed or the focus of your writing changes, you should start a new paragraph with its own point.

Second, a useful way of determining when to start a new paragraph is to use the mnemonic "Tip-Top". This stands for "Time, Place, Topic, Person". In other words, start a new paragraph whenever the time, place, topic, or person being discussed changes.

Third, citation of a whole paragraph is sometimes necessary but needed to be quoted appropriately to avoid being accused as academic misconduct. Citations in the paper and references list at the end of paper should be in consistency.

Fourth, you can proofread each paragraph backwards sentence by sentence to check grammar errors since this will help you avoid being distracted by content problems.

Activity 4 »

Directions: Work in pairs and review how to use quotations in your essay or to cite a whole paragraph without being accused of plagiarism.

Methods to avoid plagiarism (*see Chapter 1*):

1) _____

2) _____

3) _____

4) _____

Directions: Work individually and revise your rough draft.

(1) While revising, note how to revise sentences and words.

(2) Note how to revise structures, sections/chapters and paragraphs.

7 Revising Sentences

When revising, ask yourself these three questions about your sentences:

1) Are they grammatically correct?

2) Are they varied, and do they emphasize the most important information?

3) Are they as concise as they can without losing meaning or affecting style?

How to revise sentences:

Grammar mistakes should be checked sentence by sentence in this step. Proofreading is a good way to check grammar errors if you can read each sentence out loudly since it allows you to make sense of whether the words together sound fluent and meaningful.

When editing sentences, you should make sure each sentence is clear and concise. Try to avoid compound sentences and subordinate clauses unless when necessary since they may cause confusion for readers and grammar mistakes.

Punctuation is another aspect which deserves your attention when revising your rough draft. You are suggested to check punctuation errors in each sentence by asking the following questions:

- Is capital letter correctly used at the beginning of each sentence?
- Do you use a period, question mark, or exclamation point to end a sentence?
- Have you used commas, quotation marks and dashes correctly in a sentence?

Never underestimate the negative consequence of punctuation errors which may give the readers an impression that you are not very rigorous and the efforts you put in the thesis are far from enough.

In all, with all guidance for revising sentences, a rough draft can be edited into a polished work.

Activity 6 »

Directions: Work in pairs and find out the differences between the Chinese punctuation and English punctuation as much as you can.

In Chinese	In English
1. "。"	1. "."
2.	2.
3.	3.
4.	4.
5.	5.
6.	6.

Activity 7 »

Directions: Find out the punctuation and grammar errors in the following paragraphs and then discuss your findings with your partner.

"There is no great writing, only great re-writing" said Louis Brandeis. Editing your own writing is based on several times of rereading your rough draft. But is the more revisions the better? It seems that neither a student nor a busy tutor have enough time to revise a paper repeatedly. Usually, a thesis might be submitted after revision at least for three times.

Because writers often discover and develop their ideas as they draft. The draft thesis may no longer capture the writing's main idea. This might mean you should adjust your evidence match your thesis. More frequently, it means you should revise your thesis. Also check you draft, and be sure that the introduction indicate your purpose — your reasons for writing.

8 Revising Words

Words are the most fundamental but the most important elements of an academic paper. While revising the draft, make sure that your individual words and sentences reflect your ideas and attitude because every single word counts. Thus, revising each word by proofreading aims to recheck the accuracy, effectiveness, appropriateness and spelling of the word.

How to revise words:

- Be sure that each word reflects your intended meaning, having the right function. Also consider the emotional associations, or connotations, which words carry.
- Consider the level of formality that is appropriate to your writing situation. All writing benefits from avoiding biased language.
- Consider whether you have combined general and abstract language with specific and

concrete words. Explaining broad issues requires abstract language, but specific words will make your writing more compelling.

Be aware of other points while revising words:

- Avoid using snobbish words and jargon since you should make your paper easily understood rather than show off your diction ability.

- Special attention should be paid to the words relating to gender, ethnicity, and religion.

- Try to use synonyms to vary your words instead of the repetition of a same word unless it is irreplaceable.

- Never overuse adverbs and adjectives to color your sentence since preciseness and conciseness always come first in academic paper.

- Spell checkers are helpful but not perfect. Sometimes it cannot underline the misused word which is spelled correctly, so trust your own eyes rather than rely completely on spell checkers.

- Proofreading the paper backwards is helpful for checking spelling. Start checking each word separately from the end of a paper and read backwards to the beginning. For details, see the following checklist for proofreading.

拓展阅读：10.2

What and when
Second-language
Learners Revise ...

Check list for Revising and Editing

Words:
- □ Accurate diction
- □ No snobbish or big words
- □ No discriminatory words relating to gender, ethnicity and religion, etc.
- □ No overuse of adv. & adj.
- □ Correct spelling

Words:
- □ Accurate diction
- □ No snobbish or big words
- □ No discriminatory words relating to gender, ethnicity and religion, etc.
- □ No overuse of adv. & adj.
- □ Correct spelling

Words:
- □ ...

... ...

Sentence 1:
- □ Correct grammar
- □ Clear & concise sentence structure
- □ Proper punctuation

Sentence 2:
- □ Correct grammar
- □ Clear & concise sentences tructure
- □ Proper punctuation

Sentence 3: ...
Sentence 4: ...
Sentence 5: ...
Sentence 6: ...
Sentence 7: ...
...

... ...

Paragraph 1:
- □ A main point for each paragraph
- □ All sentences sticking to the main point
- □ Proper citations
- □ Tip-Top method to start a new paragraph

Paragraph 2:
- □ A main point for each paragraph
- □ All sentences sticking to the main point
- □ Proper citations
- □ Tip-Top method to start a new paragraph

Paragraph 3: ...
Paragraph 4: ...
...

... ...

- □ Main topic analyzed with multi-angles
- □ Logical order of paragraphs
- □ Content of paragraphs
- □ Transition between paragraphs
- □ Tone
- □ Tense
- □ Voice
- □ Third-person of view
- □ Authoritative expressions

... ...

Abstract

- □ Appropriate title
- □ Clear central idea
- □ Well-organized structure
- □ Correct format

Overall Structure

Introduction

Literature Review

Body parts

Conclusion

Directions: Work with your partner.

(1) Revise and edit your rough draft according to the checklist for proofreading.

(2) Discuss the mistakes/errors made in the rough draft, and then share opinions of how to correct them.

9 Self-Evaluation

For each question below, check one by one by using ticks "√" in the columns, according to your rough draft.

Questions	Yes	No	Unclear
1. Does the title indicate the central idea of the paper?			
2. Is the central idea well developed and supported?			
3. Is the structure organized properly and logically?			
4. Are all necessary parts available and related closely to the central idea?			
5. Is the format correct and proper?			
6. Are all quotations being introduced and cited correctly?			
7. Is the expression accurate, objective, concise and appropriate?			
8. Are there any grammar mistakes?			
9. Is the paper free from punctuation and spelling errors?			
10. Is the paper audience-oriented and easy to understand?			

Chapter 11
Research Proposal

In this chapter, you will know:

√ What a research proposal is,

√ Why you need to write a research proposal,

√ Elements of a research proposal,

√ How to write a research proposal.

1 Critical Thinking Questions

Directions: Work in small groups and discuss the following open questions.

■ For writing an academic paper, is a research proposal necessary or not? Why?

■ Will a research proposal be made before or after the writing of academic paper? Which way is better? And why?

■ What information should be included in a research proposal?

② Introduction to Research Proposal

Writing a research proposal is an essential step before starting a research paper if you want to apply for a degree or get funded. On the basis of discussions with tutor to select an appropriate topic and make a research plan, a research proposal should be submitted to the tutor and Thesis Supervisory Committee, to prove the significance and feasibility of the proposed research. Only if a research proposal gets approval from assessors after defense, a research project/paper can get started. Thus, a perfect proposal is a good beginning of one research paper, which promises the success of the research project or the high quality of a research paper.

Generally speaking, all the core elements and indispensable information involved in the research process should be provided in a research proposal, for the judges to evaluate the feasibility of proposed research.

Essential elements of a research proposal:

1. Title
2. Writer's information
3. Literature Review
4. Abstract
5. Significance
6. Methodology
7. Time
8. Reference Schedule
9. Table of contents
10. Introduction
11. Research background
12. Research objectives
13. Research questions
14. Innovation points
15. Acknowledgement

Despite of the differences in research areas and methodologies, all research proposals are expected to answer the core **"5Ws"** questions which are in accordance with the main components of a research proposal: **What** you are going to study (title); **Why** you want to study it (introduction); **Where** you are at levels now (literature review); **Which** ways you will apply to achieve it (methodology) and **When** you will finish it (time schedule).

Some reasons for being assigned to write a research proposal by professors:

- Develop your skills in thinking way and designing a comprehensive research study.

- Learn how to conduct a comprehensive review of the literature to ensure that a research problem has not already been answered and, in doing so, to become better at locating scholarship related to your topic.

- Improve your general research and writing skills.

- Practice identifying the logical steps that must be taken to accomplish one's research goals.

- Critically review, examine, and consider the use of different methods for gathering and analyzing data related to the research problem.

- Nurture a sense of inquisitiveness and help to see yourself as an active participant in the process of doing scholarly research.

Simply, an effective proposal should contain all the key elements involved, with sufficient information that allows readers to assess the validity and usefulness of your proposed study. The only elements missing from a research proposal are the findings of the study and your analysis of those results. Therefore, it is important that your research proposal's writing is coherent, clear, and compelling. To write an effective proposal, some common mistakes should be avoided.

Common mistakes to avoid:

- Failure to be concise; being "all over the map" without a clear sense of purpose.

- Failure to cite landmark works in your literature review.

- Failure to delimit the contextual boundaries of your research (e.g., time, place, people).

- Failure to develop a coherent and persuasive argument for the proposed research.

- Failure to stay focused on the research problem.

- Sloppy or imprecise writing, or poor grammar.

- Too much detail on minor issues, but not enough detail on major issues.

扩展阅读：11.1

Practice — How to ...
Write a research
proposal

Activity 1 »

Directions: Work with your partner, try to use the following checklist to do a peer review on your research proposal before finished, to make sure if you have addressed the questions clearly in your research proposal.

A checklist for essential elements of a research proposal:

Use "√" to tick out the elements that you think should be included in your research proposal.

☐ 1. Title

☐ 2. Writer's information

☐ 3. Literature Review

☐ 4. Abstract

☐ 5. Significance

☐ 6. Time schedule

☐ 7. Methodology

☐ 8. Reference

☐ 9. Table of contents

☐ 10. Introduction

☐ 11. Research background

☐ 12. Research objectives

☐ 13. Research questions

☐ 14. Innovation points

☐ 15. Acknowledgement

Activity 2 »

Directions: What is the right sequence of writing a research proposal? After finishing the Activity 1 above, write down the elements you have chosen in a numerical order. And then share your reasons with your partner.

3 Guidance and Structure of Writing a Research Proposal

The following table is the structure of a research proposal and the guidance of how to write it. Now, let's practice writing a research proposal by filling the form listed below; directions on how to finish each part of a research proposal are given in the form.

Title
Guidance:The title should be as accurate as you can; the wording should be thought over and polished.

Directions: Write your title here.

Abstract:

Guidance: An abstract is the first impression you leave for the readers. A good abstract is a brief statement to illustrate your answers on the "5Ws" questions by using the most concise wording in one paragraph or two to ensure the busy readers can understand you clearly. All these information of vital importance in your research should be summarized in about 200-300 words. The abstract part in your research paper may be more integrated and longer, but it can be developed on the basis of this one.

Directions: Write your sample abstract here.

Table of contents:

Guidance: The framework of your research should be listed here to provide a skeleton and a whole-view for readers although it may not be as precise as the outline of your research paper. The format of MLA or APA is strongly recommended to use here; and rules for MLA and APA can be found in Chapter 9 of this book.

Directions: Write your sample table of contents here.

Introduction:

Guidance: Introduction is the essential part of the whole research proposal since it contains the core elements including research background, research objectives & research questions, innovation points and significance. The successful arrangement of this part can lay the foundation for the approval of your research proposal.

In short, the main purpose of the introduction is to provide the necessary background or context for your research problem. The introduction typically begins with a general statement of the problem and the context, with a focus on a specific research problem, to be followed by the rationale or justification for the proposed study. Also the introduction generally states your hypothesis or theory and sets the delimitation or boundaries of your proposed research in order to provide a clear focus.

1. Research background: *Guidance: The relevant context of your proposal along with the reasons why you choose this research topic should be explained in multi-aspects in research background.*	Directions: Write your sample research background here simply.
2.Research objectives & research questions *Guidance: All the research objectives and questions should be elaborated in details along with how they are proposed based on previous hypotheses since the whole project will be built around this. Clear boundaries should be set in this part to frame the research questions and ensure the results target-oriented. Limitations of your research on the topic are also worth being mentioned if they exist.*	Directions: Describe the research questions and the purpose of the research here precisely and clearly, especially if the problems are complicated and multifaceted.
3. Innovation points *Guidance: The differences or distinctive areas of your research paper compared with others are innovation points. The value of your paper mostly depends on the innovative points.*	Directions: Describe the areas that make your research paper distinctive.

4. Significance	Directions: Write your paper's significance here briefly.
Guidance: In the significance part, the writer should state the values of your research both theoretically and practically, list the reasons why this research is worth pursuing and explain whether your research findings can contribute to the development of the relevant study areas with appropriate rationales.	

Literature review:

Guidance: Sometimes literature review may appear in the introduction section. However, most professors prefer a separate section, which allows a more thorough review of the literature.

The literature review serves several important functions:

1) *Ensure that you are not "reinventing the wheel".*

2) *Give credits to those who have laid the groundwork for your research.*

3) *Demonstrate your knowledge of the research problem.*

4) *Demonstrate your understanding of the theoretical and research issues.*

5) *Show your ability to critically evaluate relevant literature information.*

6) *Indicate your ability to integrate and synthesize the existing literature.*

7) *Provide new theoretical insights.*

A well-organized literature review can show your deep comprehension of the knowledge and theories related to your research questions, and demonstrate your ability to read, sort out, analyze, refine, evaluate and synthesize the information critically. Meanwhile, a well-organized literature review provides a map for the readers of the development history of your research area and lets them know where you are standing at and what is your exploration tendency, thus to prove your research is the supplement or development of previous researches.

Directions: Write your literature review here. If the space is not enough, please add one blank piece of paper.

Methodology

Guidance: Methodology usually includes research design, specific research methods, data collection, sampling and data analysis.

In method section, you should explain how you plan to conduct your research, identify the key sources and specific steps as well as methods you intend to use and explain how they will contribute to your analysis of the topic, thus to make your research findings valid and reliable. Qualitative analysis, quantitative analysis, questionnaires, observation, interview, experiment, field investigation and case study are methods that have been used widely and frequently in research papers, to describe how the data are collected and analyzed. What should be mentioned here is that, there is no perfect method, thus the limitations and challenges should be admitted in this section when accessing and analyzing the information no matter what methods you have applied.

Directions: Write your methodology here.

Time schedule

Guidance: In time schedule's section, you should make a clear timetable according to the research schedule step by step. Marking of the exact date is not essential, but be sure you will finish the whole project/paper before deadline.

The timetable could be arranged like:

This research project/paper is planned to start in (DD-MM-YY) and be completed in (DD-MM-YY). The specific schedule is as follows:

From…to…: Select a topic;

From…to…: Literature review;

From…to…: Abstract & Introduction;

From…to…: …

Directions: Write your time schedule here.

References

Guidance: In reference section, you should list all the literature that you cite in this research proposal chronologically by date of publication or alphabetically by author. The format requirements of MLA and APA can be found in Chapter 9 of this book. This part also shows your appreciation of the researchers whose work has laid the foundation of your research.

Directions: Write your reference list here.

Activity 3 »

Directions: Work individually to draft your research proposal entitled "*Rethinking Alternative Energy*", according to the guidance and structure of writing research proposal given above. After you have written the first draft of your proposal, check the following common errors:

扩展阅读：11.2

How to write a research proposal?

    (a) Are the sentences too long?

    (b) Are the paragraphs too long?

    (c) Is any of the writing awkward, vague, long-winded, or too informal?

    (d) Have you cited your sources each time you express an idea that is not your own?

    (e) Have you utilized the correct style for citing articles or books?

4 Put it Together

Directions: Review and write down the important points which are covered in this chapter.

    1. Reasons of writing a research proposal.

_____

_____

2. Common mistakes in writing a research proposal.

3. Structure of writing a research proposal.

4. Functions of literature review.

Chapter 12
Thesis Presentation and Publication

In this chapter, you will know:

√ Why is thesis presentation/defense necessary?

√ How do you prepare for thesis presentation?

√ How do you edit the final draft for publication?

√ What are the requirements and structures of the published academic papers?

① Critical Thinking Questions

Directions: Work in small groups and discuss the following open questions.

■ What do you need to do before thesis presentation?

■ How can we make a perfect thesis presentation?

■ What are the common features of the thesis being published?

2 Thesis Presentation

Thesis presentation, also known as thesis defense, is a dynamic and comprehensive demonstration of your research paper. Many students regard it as a heavy burden which is even more difficult than writing an academic paper. Actually, you can gain extra points for your paper through a well-prepared and wonderful demonstration. Here are the suggestions to make a good thesis presentation:

Before Presentation

1) *Figure out the requirements.*

To prepare for the thesis presentation, you should first be very clear about all the requirements. For example:

When is your turn to make it?

Where do you make the presentation?

Who is your audience?

What kind of purpose of your presentation is?

How long are you expected to spend?

Is there anything you should bring with (ID card, printed-version thesis, thumb-drive, laser pen...)?

Are there any other rules you have to follow?

In addition, a thesis presentation schedule may be sent to you ahead of time to clarify all the requirements; otherwise, it is essential to contact your thesis tutor actively to be informed with all these information.

2) *Overcome nervousness.*

It is natural if you feel nervous to make a presentation or give a talk to a group of professors and experts. Actually, they do not expect you to conduct a perfect research or write a spotless paper. Good attitude, hard work, courage of exploration and specialized knowledge which you have shown in your thesis are enough to prove that you are qualified to get a degree. So rather than to worry about your performance when making presentation, use the following effective ways to overcome nervousness and be well-prepared:

- Be clear with information in each part of your paper because professors' questions may come from abstract to quotations or appendix.

- Predict some questions that may be proposed by professors and prepare answers for those "most frequently asked questions".

- Summarize the strengths and the most important ideas that you want to impress the audience.

- Practice makes perfect. Be sure you will rehearse at least three times and tape the record each time. Improve the areas that are unsatisfactory by replaying the records. You can also time yourself in this way to ensure you can finish presentation within the given time.

- Be punctual. Arrive there half an hour earlier so that you will not be worried about traffic problems or unpredictable events and you will have sufficient time to relax yourself before presentation.

- Familiarize yourself with the facilities if possible. Copy your PPT to the computer and try the visual aids to ensure they are all running well.

- A brief introduction of yourself and the basic information about your research and paper is a good way to begin your presentation which helps you to overcome nervousness.

Activity 1 »

Directions: Review and summarize the steps of making thesis presentation. Complete the sentenes by referencing the key words given and then explain them in your own words.

Before Presentation

Step One: Figure out _____

_____

Step Two: Overcome _____

_____

During Presentation

1) *Be audience-oriented.*

When it's time to make a presentation or give a talk, always keep in mind that you should be audience-oriented. No matter what you are going to present and how you will present them, you should try your best to put the audience in their audiovisual comfort zones.

2) *Design an impressive PPT and outline.*

Except for title page and narrowing the scope, start introducing the content by using an outline to tell the audience what you are going to talk about. Usually, a basic outline includes the following aspects:

- Use an opening line that captures the attention of your audience.
- Use headings and subheadings to give the audience a clue of where you are.
- Put only the most important points on PPT. Information scattering full of screen will make you lose your audience.
- Avoid irrelevant pictures and sound effects in your PPT. Pay attention to the visual effect by using the appropriate font size, style and color throughout. Try to make the PPT clear and concise, never use dazzling pictures.
- Use the sentence statement of your main point, typically in the form of a thesis statement.
- Use two or four key points, and support your key points by evidence.
- Add transition statements to guide your audience through your presentation.
- Use a conclusion to reinforce your audience's understanding of the main ideas.
- Use a closing line or invitation to ask questions, which makes it clear to your audience.

3) *Use appropriate body language.*

- Interact with your audience by using eye contact and smiles, and other polite gestures can also facilitate the audience to get your point.

- Bear in mind that you are presenting and introducing your ideas to audience, so speak naturally like you are talking with them rather than just read the information on PPT.

- Try to speak clearly and loudly at a relative slow pace, since the sudden change of speed and intonations will arouse audience's attention.

Activity 2 »

Directions: Work with a partner, review and summarize the three steps during making thesis presentation. Complete the sentences by referencing the key words given and then explain them in your own words.

During Presentation

Step One: Be _____

_____

_____

_____

_____

Step Two: Design_____

_____

_____

_____

_____

Step three: Use_____

_____

_____

_____

_____

_____

After Presentation: Q&A Session

There will be a question & answer session right after your presentation. Students always regard it as the most difficult part because the questions are usually unpredictable and need immediate responses. Though you may not come up with perfect answers, you can still perform confidently and objectively by referencing the following suggestions.

1) *Listen to the questions carefully.*

Maybe you are too nervous to focus your attention on the questions after Q&A session. If this happens, do not hesitate to ask the assessors to repeat their questions again, since requesting for repetition is better than giving irrelevant answers. However, too many repetition requests may indicate that you are absent-minded and do not have a deep understanding on the topic.

2) *Say "thank you for your question" before offering an answer as a good manner.*

You can give a quick response to the simple questions and you are also suggested to think over a complicated question for a few seconds before providing your feedback objectively.

3) *Answer questions loudly, logically and confidently.*

For every question, you should answer at a relative slow pace, and numbering your explanations in sequence will help to clarify your thoughts.

4) *Confess frankly those that are the areas which deserve your further efforts.*

For the questions you cannot come up with an answer, or the doubts and criticism on the weakness of your paper, confess frankly. Explanations are essential sometimes but irrational argument will irritate the assessors. After all, they just want to help improving your paper rather than criticizing you.

Besides the suggestions above, you are strongly recommended to *be formally dressed*. Mini-skirts, sneakers, exaggerated jewelries and jeans with broken holes are obviously inappropriate for this kind of formal occasion. Avoid bright colors and fashionable elements. Tuxedos or skirt suits will make you look more mature and professional. A clean and tidy image may not only leave the audience a good impression but may also bring you extra points and good luck!

扩展阅读：12.1

Effective
presentation skills

Activity 3 ≫

Directions: Review and summarize the steps after making thesis presentation. Complete the sentences by referencing the key words given and then explain them in your own words.

After Presentation

Step One: Listen _____

_____

_____

Step Two: Say _____

_____

Step Three: Answer _____

_____

_____

Step Four: Confess _____

_____

_____

Activity 4 ≫

Directions: Work in a small group and make a thesis presentation to other group members according to the suggestions given above. Your presentation should be given in the PowerPoint form.

Good morning, ladies and gentlemen. I would like to use this precious opportunity to present the ideas in my thesis…

3 Preparing for Publication

Publishing an academic paper is very important if you want to step into the academic community and build up your academic reputation. Usually, preparing to publish one paper is as follows:

扩展阅读：12.2

What should I do if I want to publish a paper?

■ To publish a paper, you should first polish it repeatedly to make it qualified to be circulated. Check carefully the reference format and the title page. The title page follows a standard format, such as APA Style Manual. Notice the following example of the title page in one research paper.

Political Discourse i	Shortened title or running head, is included on every page. Use Roman numerals (i, ii) for the title page; Use Arabic numbers (1,2,3) on all other pages.
Political Discourse in the Media	Title with no underline, quotation marks or italics. Perfectly centered on the page.
Authored by: Lili Wang Submitted to: Professor Barry William King's College	Clarification of author, reader, and school. Four spaces below title and centered.
Submission date: May 10, 2019	Date with three spaces below.

- Read academic journals related to your study areas and choose suitable ones for your topic and writing style; this will increase your chances of publication and help you gain wider recognition.

- Tailor your paper according to the requirements of the chosen journal. Be clear about the format, layout, font style and word limits.

- Send your paper to only one of the chosen journals at one time by using one appropriate way.

- Wait patiently for reply. Contact the editors actively if you have not got any reply after one month.

  Possible replies from journal editors would be:

- "Accept" — express your gratitude and appreciation to editors;
- "Accept with Revision" — only minor adjustments are needed, based on the provided feedback by the reviewers;
- "Revise and Resubmit" — more substantial changes are needed before publication, but the journal is still very interested in your paper;
- "Reject" — the paper is not and won't be suitable for this publication, but that doesn't mean it might not work for another journal.

- Never give up getting your paper published. Even though you are rejected by your favored journal, keep tailoring your paper and submit it to other journals. Sometimes a rejected paper should not be marked as an unqualified paper. Move on to your second-choice and third-choice journal for submission. Remember, keep trying and never give up, your paper will be recognized and published finally.

Activity 5 »

Directions: Find out and write down the names of three journals in your study area, and then list and compare their publication requirements.

_____
_____
_____
_____

Activity 6 »

Directions: Try to find a One Button Studio and record your presentation. After that, please evaluate your performance by replaying the video again and again. You can make progress by self-check like this.

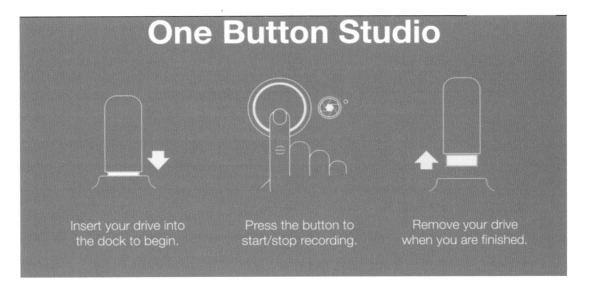

The One Button Studio

| Insert your drive into the dock to begin. | Press the button to start/stop recording. | Remove your drive when you are finished. |

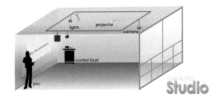

The One Button Studio is a simplified video recording setup that can be used without any previous video production experience. The design of the studio allows you to create high-quality and polished video projects without having to know anything about lights and cameras. You only need to bring your flash drive with you and push a single button.

4   Self-Evaluation

Directions: Review and write down the important points which are covered in this chapter.

1. Steps before presentation.

_____

_____

_____

_____

_____

2. Steps during presentation.

_____

_____

_____

_____

_____

3. Steps after presentation.

_____

_____

_____

_____

_____

4. Main points of publication.

_____

_____

_____

_____

_____

Appendix 1
APA Style

扩展阅读：
APA Style & Citation (6ᵗʰ ed)

APA stands for *American Psychological Association* and is a common formatting style for essays and papers in the social sciences. When using APA style, in-text citations and references in a reference list at the end of the paper should be used to provide details to identify and retrieve the sources you have used in your paper. In-text citations will use the author's name and the date in your text. These citations should be referred back to the reference list, which lists all the sources that you may have used in your research paper.

The following steps illustrate how to cite sources within the text by using the APA style.

Citations Within Text/Paper

Anytime you summarize, paraphrase or quote information from another source, like passages from books or articles in an academic journal, you are required to list the author's name, the year when the article was published and sometimes the page or location of the information, which is called the in-text citation.

APA in-text citations use an author-date form to acknowledge the use of another writer's words, facts, or ideas. When you refer to a source, please insert a parenthetical note that gives the author's last name and the year of publications, separated by a comma. The pages of quotations are sometimes included in the parentheses. Note that the APA style requires using past tense or present perfect tense to introduce the cited materials. Usually, citations within the text/paper are as follows:

1. *Basic Format for Direct Quotation*

If you are directly quoting from a source, you will need to include *the author, the year published*, and *the page number for the reference* (preceded by "p."), placing the author's last name followed by the date of publication in parentheses and then the page number in parentheses after your quotation.

E.g.

- Caruth (1996) stated that a traumatic response frequently entailed a "delayed, uncontrolled repetitive appearance of hallucinations and other intrusive phenomena" (p. 11).

If the author's name hasn't been mentioned with a signal phrase, then you need to include the author's last name, the publication date and the page number in parentheses.

E.g.

- ... stating that a traumatic response frequently entails a "delayed, uncontrolled repetitive appearance of hallucinations and other intrusive phenomena" (Caruth, 1996, p. 90).

2. *Basic Format for Summaries and Paraphrases*

If you are summarizing or paraphrasing information from other sources, include the author and year published. You're also encouraged to include the page numbers of the original information although it is not mandatory.

E.g.

- The format citation of APA style is difficult for the beginners (Jones, 1998, p. 199).
- Jones (1998) stated that the format of the APA style was difficult for the beginners (p.199).

3. *Single Author*

When citing a work or paper with only one author, you will need to include the author and the year published. If necessary, you can add page number. Usually, parenthetical citations look like this: *Author's Last name, Year, Page number if quote.*

- A recent study found a possible genetic cause of alcoholism (Pauling, 2005).
- Pauling (2005) discovered a possible genetic cause of alcoholism.

4. *Two Authors*

When citing a work with two authors, use "and" in between authors' name in the signal phrase, but use "&" between their names in parenthesis.

E.g.

- Rowling and Cramer (2005) argued for the development of new curricula.
- The development of new curricula has been argued before (Rowling & Cramer, 2005).

5. *Three to Five Authors*

When citing a work with three to five authors, place the authors in the order they appear in the source. Include all names in the signal phrase or in parenthesis at the first time. In subsequent citations, only use the first author's last name followed by "et al." in the signal phrase or in parenthesis.

E.g.

- Harklau, Siegal, and Losey (2005) discovered a possible genetic cause of alcoholism.
- A recent study found a possible genetic cause of alcoholism (Harklau, Siegal, & Losey, 2005).
- Pauling et al. (2005) discovered a possible genetic cause of alcoholism.

- A recent study found a possible genetic cause of alcoholism (Pauling et al., 2005).

6. *Six or More Authors*

When citing a work with six or more authors, identify the first author's name followed by "et al.".

E.g.

- Jones et al. (1998) argued that the format of the APA style was difficult for the beginners.
- A recent study found a possible genetic cause of alcoholism (Pauling et al., 2005).

7. *Group Author*

Write out the full name of the group or organization in the first citation and place the abbreviation next to it in brackets.

E.g.

- World Health Organization (WHO) reported that… (2002).
- A recent study found a possible genetic cause of alcoholism (World Health Organization [WHO], 2002).

8. *No Authors Listed*

When the source lacks an author's name, place the source's full title in the signal phrase and cite the first word of the title followed by the year of publication in parenthesis. Put titles of articles and chapters in quotation marks; italicize titles of books and reports.

E.g.

- According to *"Building Support Networks for the Elderly"* (2015), …
- … (*"Building"*, 2015).

Entries Cited in the Reference List

The reference list begins on a new page at the end of your paper. Alphabetize the list entries by the last name of the first author of each work. If there are multiple articles of the same author or authors in the same order, the entries should be listed in chronological order (from the earliest one to the most recent one).

The following examples illustrate the most common ways of citing sources in the *Reference List*.

Types of Sources	Formats & Examples
Book with One Author	**Format:** Author's Last name, First initial. Middle initial. (Year Published).*Title*. Location: Publisher.
	Example: ● Harmer, J. (2015). *The Practice of English Language Teaching*. Essex: Pearson Education.
Book with Two or More Authors	**Format:** The first author's Last name, First initial. Middle initial., the second author's Last name, First initial. Middle initial., & the third author's Last name, First initial. Middle initial. (Year Published). *Title*. Location: Publisher.
	Example: ● Karsh, E., & Fox, A. S. (2014). *The Only Grant-Writing Book You'll Ever Need*. New York: Basic Books.
Edited Book with an Editor	**Format:** Editor's Last name, First initial. Middle initial. (Year Published). *Title*. Location: Publisher.
	Example: ● Bailey, W.G. (Ed.). (1990). *Guide to Popular U.S. Government Publications*. Englewood, CO: Libraries Unlimited.
Journal Article	**Format:** Author's Last name, First initial. Middle initial. (Year Published). Title of article. *Title of Journal, Volume* (Issue), page range.
	Example: ● Olsher, D.(2014). Semantically-Based Priors and Nuanced Knowledge Core for Big Data, Social AI, and Language Understanding. *Neural Networks*, 58, 131-147.
Newspaper Article	**Format:** Author's Last name, First initial. Middle initial. (Year, Month Day Published). Title of article. *Name of Newspaper*, page range.
	Example: ● Lohr, S. (2004, December 3). Health Care Technology Is a Promise Unfinanced. *The New York Times*, p. C5.

(Continued)

Types of Sources	Formats & Examples
E-Journal Article	**Format:** Author's Last name, First initial. Middle initial. (Year published). Title of article. *Title of Journal*, *Volume* (Issue), pp-pp. doi:xx.xxxxxxxxxx [OR] Retrieved from URL of publication's home page
	Example: ● Sillick, T. J., & Schutte, N. S. (2006). Emotional Intelligence and Self-Esteem Mediate Between Perceived Early Parental Love and Adult Happiness. *E-Journal of Applied Psychology*, 22(2), 38-48. Retrieved from http://ojs.lib.swin.edu.au/index.php/ejap
Government Document	**Format:** Government Department (Year published). *Document title* (a series or report number). Location: Publisher.
	Example: ● Federal Aviation Administration (2004). *Seaplane, Skiplane, and Float/Ski Equipped Helicopter Operations Handbook* (FAA-H-8083-23). Washington, D.C: U.S. G.P.O.
Websites	**Format:** Author's Last Name, First initial. (Year, Month Date Published). Title of webpage. Retrieved from URL
	Example: ● Austerlitz, S. (2015, March 3). How Long Can a Spin off Like "Better Call Saul" Last? Retrieved from http://fivethirtyeight.com/features/how-long-can-a-spinoff-like-better-call-saul-last/

扩展阅读：

Publication Manual of the American Psychological Association (6th ed)

Appendix 2
MLA Style

扩展阅读：

MLA Handbook (*8th ed*)

MLA stands for *Modern Language Association* and is a common formatting style for classroom instruction and used worldwide by scholars, journal publishers, and academic and commercial presses. When you're borrowing information from a source and placing it in your research or assignment, it is important to give credit to the original author. Depending on the type of information you're including in your work, in-text citations in the body of your research paper and the corresponding entries in the *Works Cited List* at the end of the paper should be included to document the source of your information.

The following steps illustrate how to cite sources within the text by using MLA style.

Citations within Text/Paper

Like the in-text citations in the APA style, the citation in MLA is also a brief reference in your paper indicating the source you quote. In this parenthetical style, the in-text citation is enclosed in parentheses, including the author's last name and the page of the information; and more complete documentation are referred at the end of the paper. The parenthetical style in MLA helps to lead the readers to the corresponding entries in the list of *Works Cited* at the end of the paper.

1. *Basic Format for Direct Quotation*

If you are directly quoting from a source and have named the author within your sentence, include only the page number in parentheses after the quotation. When the author's name hasn't been mentioned in your sentence, the author's name and the page number in parentheses must be placed after the quotation. The period follows the parentheses.

E.g.

- Caruth stated that a traumatic response frequently entailed a "delayed, uncontrolled repetitive appearance of hallucinations and other intrusive phenomena" (11).
- A traumatic response frequently entails a "delayed, uncontrolled repetitive appearance of hallucinations and other intrusive phenomena" (Caruth 11).

2. *Basic Format for Summaries and Paraphrases*

Parenthetical citation must also be used when you are summarizing or paraphrasing information from a source. If the author's name is mentioned in the text, then place only the page number in parentheses after the summary or paraphrase. Punctuation marks follow the parentheses. If you have not mentioned the author in your sentence, you must place the author's name and page number in parentheses after the quotation.

E.g.

- Jones believes that the citation format of APA style is difficult for beginners (199).
- The citation format of APA style is difficult for first-time beginners (Jones 199).

3. *One Author*

When citing a work with one author, the author's name may appear either in the sentence or in the parentheses after the quotation. But always put the page number in the parentheses.

E.g.

- Wordsworth stated that Romantic poetry was featured by a "spontaneous overflow of powerful feelings" (263).
- Romantic poetry is featured by a "spontaneous overflow of powerful feelings" (Wordsworth 263).

4. *Two Authors*

When citing a work with two authors, use "and" to connect the authors' names, including the last name of each authors in your citation.

E.g.

- As Gostin and Gostin explain, "Interventions that do not pose a truly significant on individual liberty ... go a long way towards safeguarding the health and well-being"(214).
- Interventions that do not pose a truly significant on individual liberty ... go a long way towards safeguarding the health and well-being (Gostin & Gostin 214).

5. *Three or More Authors*

Only use the first author's last name followed by "et al." (Latin for "and others"). Note that there is no comma between the author's name and "et al."

E.g.

- A traumatic response frequently entails a "delayed, uncontrolled repetitive appearance of hallucinations and other intrusive phenomena" (Caruth et al. 117).

6. *Corporate, Group or Government Author*

Write out the full name of the group or organization in the first citation and place the abbreviation next to it in parentheses. Then you may use abbreviations for the source in the subsequent references.

E.g.

- World Health Organization (WHO) finds that more countries have implemented tobacco control policies (22). WHO also mentions that about 5 billion people, 65% of the world's population, are covered by at least one comprehensive tobacco control measure (46).

7. *No Authors Listed*

When the source lacks an author's name, use the first one, two, or three words from the title. Don't count initial articles like "A", "An" or "The". Enough words should be provided to make it clear which work you're referring to from your *Works Cited List*.

E.g.

- ... (*New York Public* 177).

8. *Two or More Works by the Same Author*

If you are quoting from an author whose two or more works are in the *Works Cited List*, insert a short version of the title between author and page number, separating the author and the title with a comma.

E.g.

- ... (Wee, *Resurrecting* 60).
- ... (Wee, *Scream* 47).

9. *Two or More Works Cited Together*

When two or more works are cited together within the text, use a semicolon to separate entries.

E.g.

- Global warming is small and magnified by the alarmists with deeply compromised political pressure, data fudging, and out guesswork (Estes and Otte 2; Wither and Hosking 144; Wee 60).

Entries in the Works Cited List

The MLA style research documentation includes a reference list titled "Works Cited List". The list begins on a new page at the end of your paper. Alphabetize the list entries by the last name of the first author of each work. If there are multiple articles of the same author, the entries should be listed alphabetically by title and three hyphens in place of the author's name should be used for every entry after the first.

The following examples illustrate the most common ways of citing sources in the *Works*

Cited List.

Types of Sources	Formats & Examples
Book with an Author	**Format:** Author's Last name, First name. *Title of Book*. Publisher, Year Published.
	Example: ● Harmer, Jeremy. *The Practice of English Language Teaching*. Pearson Education, 2015.
Book with Two Authors	**Format:** The first author's Last name, First name, and the second author's First name, Last name. *Title of Book*. Publisher, Year Published.
	Example: ● Gillespie, Paula, and Neal Lerner. *The Allyn and Bacon Guide to Peer Tutoring*. Allyn and Bacon, 2000.
Book with Three or More Authors	**Format:** The first author's Last name, First name, et al. *Title of Book*. Publisher, Year Published.
	Example: ● Campbell, Megan, et al. *The Best Noun Book*. Books For Us, 2017.
Book by a Corporate Author or Organization	**Format:** Full name of the cooperation or group. *Title of Book*. Publisher, Year Published.
	Example: ● National Fire Protection Association. *Fundamentals of Fire Fighting Skills*. Jones and Bartlett, 2009.
Book with Editor(s)	**Format:** Author's Last name, First name, editor. *Title of Book*. Numbered ed., Publisher, Year published.
	Example: ● Leonard, William and Michael Crawford, editors. *Human Biology of Pastoral Populations*. 1st ed.,Cambridge University Press, 2003.
E-Books	**Format:** Author's Last name, First name. *Title of E-Book*. Publisher, Year published. Title of Website, URL.

(Continued)

Types of Sources	Formats & Examples
E-Books	**Example:** ● Rodgers, Tara. *Pink Noises: Women on Electronic Music and Sound.* Duke UP, 2010. Google Books, books.google.com/books?id=syqTar qO5XEC&lpg=PP1&dq=electronic%20 music&pg=PP1#v=onepage &q=electronic%20 music&f=false.
Journal Article	**Format:** Author's last name, first name. "Article Title." *Title of Journal*, Volume, Issue, Date, Pages. **Example:** ● Zak, Elizabeth. "Do You Believe in Magic? Exploring the Conceptualization of Augmented Reality and Its Implications for the User in the Field of Library and Information Science." *Information Technology & Libraries*, vol. 33, No. 3, 12 Nov. 2014, pp. 23-50.
Newspaper Article	**Format:** Author's name. "Title of Article." *Title of Newspaper*, Date, Page(s). **Example:** ● Lohr, Smith. "Health Care Technology Is a Promise Unfinanced." *New York Times*, 3 Dec, 2004, C5.
E-Journal Article	**Format:** Author's last name, first name. "Article Title." *Title of Journal*, Volume, Issue, Date: Pages. Database name. URL or DOI. **Example:** ● Butte, G. "Henry James and Deep Intersubjectivity." *The Henry James Review*, vol. 30, No. 2, 2009, pp. 129-143. Project MUSE. doi:10.1353/hjr.0.0045.
Websites	**Format:** Contributor's Last name, First name. "Title of Web Page." *Title of Website*, Website Publisher, Date, URL, Date of Access. **Example:** ● Fosslien, Liz, and Mollie West. "3 Ways to Hack Your Environment to Help You Create." *Huffpost Preposition Endeavor*, Huffington Post, Dec. 7, 2016, www.huffingtonpost.com/entry/3-ways-to-hack- your-environment-to-help-you-createus580f758be4b02444efa569bc.

Appendix 3
Chicago Style

扩展阅读:

The Chicago Manual of Style (17ᵗʰ edition)

The Chicago Manual of Style (CMOS) is a formatting style commonly used in the field of literature, history, and arts. There are two different documentation styles in CMOS: the *Notes-Bibliography* system, which uses footnotes and endnotes, and the *Author-Date* system, which uses parenthetical citations within the text itself. Before writing, you may decide at first whether to use endnote or footnote. Footnotes are added directly at the bottom of the pages containing the corresponding numbers that are after your referenced sources, while endnotes can usually be found in a separate page entitled "*Notes*"after the text and before the bibliography page.

This appendix deals with the *Notes-Bibliography* system.

Citations Within the Text/Paper

In *Notes-Bibliography* system, notes are used for in-text citations to cite sources and to provide relevant commentary. A bibliography page, including all sources cited within notes and sometimes other relevant sources that are not cited but provide further reading, should be added at the end of your paper.

The following steps illustrate how to cite sources within the text by using Chicago *Notes-Bibliography* system.

1. *Numbering*

To cite from sources, notes should be numbered consecutively throughout your work, beginning with 1, which is placed after the quotes or paraphrases. Those citation numbers must be in sequential order. Each number corresponds to a citation, a footnote or an endnote.

2. *Placing the Note Numbers in the Text*

Place the number for a note at the end of the sentence containing the reference after punctuation and outside any parenthesis. Also the note number should precede the dash if you are citing the sources that come before an dash. Note numbers are set as superscripts.

E.g.

● In Democracy and Other Neoliberal Fantasies, Jodi Dean argues that "imagining a rhizome might be nice, but rhizomes don't describe the underlying structure of real networks,"[1] rejecting the idea…

- Michael Hardt and Antonio Negri, on the other hand, argue that the Internet is an exemplar of the rhizome: a nonhierarchical, concentered network[2] — a democratic network with "an indeterminate and potentially unlimited number of interconnected nodes that communicate with no central point of control."[3]

3. *Including Page Numbers in a Note*

Use page numbers whenever you refer to a specific page of a source rather than to the source as a whole. Using page numbers is required for quotations.

E.g.

- ... Rinker Buck stated: "A new American journey began ..."[1], 92.

4. *Cross-Reference Notes*

If you are referring to a source identified in a previous note, you can refer to that note instead of repeating the information.

E.g.

- ... (See note 3 above.)

> **Notes and Entries in Bibliography or Worked Cited List**

The Chicago Manual of Style provides guideline for formatting notes and entries in a bibliography, appearing at the end of the document. The first time you cite a source, the footnote or the endnote will look very similar to a full bibliography entry because all relevant information should be listed about that source. Pay attention to the slight differences. If the same source is cited two or more times consecutively, you could use shortened notes.

The bibliographic ***notes*** are listed alphabetically, include these elements:

- author's name (first name first)
- title
- date
- publisher
- page being cited

The bibliographic ***entries*** are listed alphabetically, include these elements:

- author's name (last name first)
- title
- date
- publisher

● page being cited

The following examples illustrate the most common ways of notes and entries in the *Bibliography*.

Types of Sources	Examples
Book with an Author	**Note:** 1. Jeremy Harmer, *The practice of English Language Teaching* (Essex: Pearson Education, 2015), 15. **Shortened Note:** 2. Harmer, *The Practice*, 20. **Bibliography Entry:** Harmer, Jeremy. *The practice of English Language Teaching*. Essex: Pearson Education, 2015.
Book with Two Authors	**Note:** 1. Paula Gillespie and Neal Lerner, *The Allyn and Bacon Guide to Peer Tutoring* (Boston: Allyn and Bacon, 2000), 27-29. **Shortened Note:** 2. Gillespie and Lerner, *The Allyn and Bacon Guide to Peer Tutoring*, 50. **Bibliography Entry:** Gillespie, Paula, and Neal Lerner. *The Allyn and Bacon Guide to Peer Tutoring*. Boston: Allyn and Bacon, 2000.
Book with Editor(s)	**Note:** 1. Adelaida R. Del Castillo, ed., *Between Borders: Essays on Mexicana/Chicana History* (Encino, CA: Floricanto, 1990), 212-56. **Shortened Note:** 2. Del Castillo, *Between Borders*, 234. **Bibliography Entry:** Del Castillo, Adelaida R., ed. *Between Borders: Essays on Mexicana/Chicana History*. Encino, CA: Floricanto, 1990.

(Continued)

Types of Sources	Examples
E-Books	**Note:** 1. Herman Melville, *Moby-Dick; or, The Whale* (New York: Harper & Brothers, 1851), 627, http://mel.hofstra.edu/moby-dick-the-whale-proofs.html.
E-Books	**Shortened Note:** 2. Melville, *Moby-Dick*, 521–23. **Bibliography Entry:** Melville, Herman. *Moby-Dick; or, The Whale*. New York: Harper & Brothers, 1851. http://mel.hofstra.edu/moby-dick-the-whale-proofs.html.
Journal Article	**Note:** 1. Susan Peck MacDonald, "The Erasure of Language," *College Composition and Communication* 58, no. 4 (2007): 588. **Shortened Note:** 2. MacDonald, "The Erasure of Language," 601. **Bibliography Entry:** MacDonald, Susan Peck. "The Erasure of Language." *College Composition and Communication* 58, no. 4 (2007): 583-620.
Newspaper Article	**Note:** 1. Rebecca Mead, "The Prophet of Dystopia," *New Yorker*, April 17, 2017, 43. **Shortened Note:** 2. Mead, "Dystopia," 47. **Bibliography Entry:** Mead, Rebecca. "The Prophet of Dystopia." *New Yorker*, April 17, 2017.

(Continued)

Types of Sources	Examples
E-Journal Article	**Note:** 1.Gueorgi Kossinets and Duncan J. Watts, "Origins of Homophily in an Evolving Social Network," *American Journal of Sociology* 115 (2009): 420, accessed December 5, 2014, doi:10.1086/599247. **Shortened Note:** 2. Kossinets and Watts, "Origins of Homophily," 450. **Bibliography Entry:** Kossinets, Gueorgi, and DuncanJ. Watts. "Origins of Homophily in an Evolving Social Network." *American Journal of Sociology* 115 (2009): 409-50. Accessed December5, 2014. doi:10.1086/599247.
Websites	**Note:** 1. "About Yale: Yale Facts," Yale University, accessed May 1, 2017, https://www.yale.edu/about-yale/yale-facts. **Shortened Note:** 2. "Yale Facts." **Bibliography Entry:** Yale University. "About Yale: Yale Facts." Accessed May 1, 2017. https://www.yale.edu/about-yale/yale-facts.

References

[1] Alice Oshima & Ann Hogue (2006). *Writing Academic English* (Fourth Edition). New York: Pearson Education Press.

[2] American Psychological Association (2009). *Manual of the American Psychological Association* (*6th ed.*).Washington, DC: American Psychological Association.

[3] American Psychological Association (2010). *Concise rules of APA style* (*6th ed.*). Washington, DC: American Psychological Association.

[4] Bhutan (2009). A Students Guide to Academic Writing and Referencing and Documentation(D). Paro College of Education, Royal University of Bhutan.

[5] Boud David, Ruth Chen & Jane Sampson (1999). "Peer Learning and Assessment." *Assessment and Evaluation in Higher Education*, 24: 413-426.

[6] Carole Slade & Robert Perrin (2010). *Handbook for Writing Research Papers, Reports and Theses* (*Thirteenth Edition*). Beijing: Foreign Language Teaching and Research Press.

[7] Cogie Jane, Kim Strain & Sharon Lorinskas (1999). "Avoiding the Proofreading Trap: The Value of the Error Correction Process." *The Writing Center Journal*, 19 : 7-32.

[8] Claudia Steinkuhl, M.A. & Clare Gray (2009). *Academic Writing Handbook* (D). University of Applied Sciences Osnabrueck.

[9] Derek Soles (2009). *The Essentials of Academic Writing* (*2nd edition*). Cambridge, MA: Wadsworth Publishing.

[10] Ding Wangdao, et (2009). *A Handbook of Writing* (*Third Edition*). Beijing: Foreign Language Teaching and Research Press.

[11] Dorothy E. Zemach, Daniel Broudy & Chris Valvona (2015). *Writing Research Papers*. Beijing: Foreign Language Teaching and Research Press.

[12] Dorothy Zemach & Lisa A Rumisek (2009). *Academic Writing from Paragraph to Essay*. London: Macmillan Press.

[13] Dorothy E. Zemach (2004). *Paragraph Writing: from Sentence to Paragraph*. London: Macmillan ELT.

[14] Els Van Geyte (2013). *Writing: Learn To Write Better Academic Essays* (*English For Academic Purposes*). New York: HarperCollins.

[15] Gail Craswell & Megan Poore (2011). *Writing for Academic Success*. London: SAGE Publications Ltd.

[16] Ji Chenghui (2008). *An Advanced Cource for English Writing*. Beijing: Foreign Language Teaching and Research Press.

[17] Joan McCormack & John Slaght (2006). *English for Academic Study: Extended Writing and Research Skills*. Beijing: Higher Education Press.

[18] John M. Swales & Christine B. Feak (2012). *Academic Writing for Graduate Students: Essential Tasks and Skills* (*3rd Edition*). Michigan: University of Michigan Press, ELT.

[19] John Langan (2011). *College writing skills* (*8th edition*). New York: McGraw-Hill Companies, Inc.

[20] Martin Hewings (2012). *Cambridge Academic English: An Integrated Skills Course Book 2* (*2nd* Edition). London: Cambridge University Press.

[21] Madraso, Jan (1993). "Proofreading: The Skill We've Neglected to Teach." *The English Journal*, 82(2): 32-41.

[22] Mike Palmquist (2017). *The Bedford Researcher* (*6th edition*). Bsoton / New York: Bedford/St. Martin's, Macmillan Learning.

[23] Modern Language Association (2016). *MLA Handbook* (*8th ed.*). New York: The Modern Language Association of America.

[24] Oliver, P (2007). *Writing your thesis*. New Delhi: Vistaar Publication.

[25] Rowena Murray and Sarah Moore (2011). *The Handbook of Academic Writing A Fresh Approach*. New York: McGraw-Hill Companies, Inc.

[26] Stephanie Ken (March 29, 2019). *How to Edit Your Own Writing* [OL]. Retrieved from https://www.wikihow.com.

[27] Stephen Bailey (2015). *The Essentials of Academic Writing for International Students*. London: Routledge.

[28] Stephen Bailey (2017). *Academic Writing: A Handbook for International Students* (*English Edition*). London: Routledge.

[29] Stephen Lucas (2015). *The Art of Public Speaking* (12th edition). Boston: McGraw-Hill Higher Education.

[30] Tang, R (2014). *Academic Writing in a Second or Foreign Language: Issues and Challenges Facing ESL/EFL Academic*. London: Bloomsbury Academic References.

[31] Thomas S. Kane (2000). *Essential Guide to Writing*. New York: Berkley Books.

[32] University Writing Center, Texas A&M University. (May 26, 2019). *There Is No Great Writing,Only Great Re-writing [OL]*. http://writingcenter.tamu.edu/.

[33] University of Southern California (April 23rd, 2019). *Organizing Your Social Sciences Research Paper: Proofreading Your Paper[OL]*. http://libguides.usc.edu/writingguide/proofreading.

[34] University of Chicago (2003). *The Chicago Manual of Style* (*15th ed.*). Chicago: University of Chicago Press.

[35] William Strunk (2016). *The Elements of Style*. Beijing: Foreign Language Teaching and Research Press.

[36] Wang Yulei (2017). *A Guide to Academic Research Paper Writing and Publishing*. Beijing: Renmin University of China Press.

[37] Wang Xianhong (2008). Academic Document Retrieving. Beijing: China Financial and Economic Publishing House.

[38] Yang Xinliang & Xiong Yan (2012). *Academic English Writing*. Shanghai: Shanghai Jiao Tong University Press.

教师服务

感谢您选用清华大学出版社的教材！为了更好地服务教学，我们为授课教师提供本书的教学辅助资源，以及本学科重点教材信息。请您扫码获取。

≫ 教辅获取

本书教辅资源，授课教师扫码获取

≫ 样书赠送

公共基础课类重点教材，教师扫码获取样书

 清华大学出版社

E-mail: tupfuwu@163.com
电话：010-83470332 / 83470142
地址：北京市海淀区双清路学研大厦 B 座 509

网址：https://www.tup.com.cn/
传真：8610-83470107
邮编：100084